LIVE WITH YOUR PET IN MIND

Dr. Jodie
Integrative Veterinarian

To Beth -
Thank you for your
devotion to natural
health & passion
for pets!
♡ Dr. Jodie

Live with Your Pet in Mind

The content of this book is for general instruction only. Each person's and pet's physical, emotional, and spiritual condition is unique. The instruction in this book is not intended to replace or interrupt the reader's relationship with a physician or other veterinary professional. Please consult your doctor or your pet's veterinarian for matters pertaining to your specific health, diet and that of your pet. In some cases, pet or guardian names have been changed to protect their privacy.

For additional information visit: **www.DrJodiesNaturalPets.com**

ISBN-13: 978-1536833515
ISBN-10: 1536833517
Printed in the United States of America

About the cover artist
LaVonna Moore is an author, writer, and book cover designer. LaVonna enjoys photography and working in her orchard in the country. LaVonna is an animal lover. She has a calico kitty named Callie, a Great Pyrenees named Angel, a cockatiel named Anna, a canary named Lucy, and a parakeet named LuLu.
http://www.selfpubbookcovers.com/VonnaArt

DEDICATION

This book is a tribute to Rebecca Moravec, an Animal Communicator and Kindred Spirit

When Rebecca told me, that Mork said, "*I am worried about my mom. She is so busy! When we get home, she rushes around making our food, and then she plops down on the couch, and watches TV and eats!*", I knew Rebecca was real, that Mork cared, and that I needed to change! When Mork saw, that Rebecca had noticed, Snoopy lifting his leg on the bookcase, and Mork said to her, "*I don't do that.*" I knew *he* was talking. I didn't think my relationship with animals could have gotten any deeper, until Rebecca told me how *they* felt.

Rebecca, you are greatly missed.

Although she has passed, to honor Rebecca, you may still visit her website:
http://www.kindredspiritsanimalcommunication.com

CONTENTS

ACKNOWLEDGEMENTS AND APPRECIATION

Jesus
For being with me even before and after my mom
taught me to pray, "Dear Jesus, Thank You for this day..."

Mom, Dad for the all-time influence
Lindsay for the present and for being my everything
Bob for the formative past

Kati Gingras, CVT
For project assistance, pet sitting and being my right arm
Joyce Paisley for flattering photos and back cover design
Melody Carranza for a most memorable photograph

Lorraine R. Causing for darling illustrations

Pamela Anderson for impeccable copy editing

Julanne Denome for friendship and emotional support

Clients, Pet Patients, My Own Pets
For the stories

Colleagues, Co-workers, Instructors
For the support and education

Face Book Friends and Followers
For the sharing and the "likes"

Life development: Integrative Nutrition® and IIN®
Trademarks by Integrative Nutrition Inc. with permission

i

FOREWORD

LIVE WITH YOUR PET IN MIND is a hidden treasure for true holistic care for your pets. The book is organized in a manner that is easy to understand, simple to use and effective. In addition to instruction on the overall health of your pet, including essential oil application, the book incorporates the use of thought and word power.

A wise teacher uses many stories and that is what Dr. Jodie has so eloquently done in guiding the reader through her life experiences and clinical applications. We see an amazing correlation in the health of the pet guardian and the pets. The reader is educated and made aware of the primary needs and top health concerns for their animals and for themselves.

Dr. Jodie shares insights into how to take better care of ourselves and our pets. She recommends identify, avoid and or replace the toxic foods that we are eating and often, unknowingly, feeding to our animals. Our thoughts and words are manifesting in our daily habits and lifestyle. Our animals are taking on our stuff, through their emotional connections to us, and their physical existence in our space.

I think the most important message in Dr. Jodie's book is her authenticity and true caring for you as a human being and the animals you love and care for. A true picture of holistic, healthy pet care is summarized from our thoughts to our actions. Our animals depend on us for their emotional care, food, and water, grooming and general medical care. Dr. Jodie shares in her stories how we are communicating with them through our own natural instincts. Make the wisdom of this book your essential companion as it reveals the keys necessary to unlock the knowledge of true mind, body and spirit pet and self-care.

~ Marcella Vonn Harting, PhD~
Psychoneurology & Integrative Health
Author "Yes, No, Maybe" Chronobiotic Nutrition" and"Guerrilla MultiLevel
Marketing

For GOD did not give us a spirit of timidity,

but a spirit of power, of love, and of self-discipline.

2 Timothy 1:7 Birth Verse

He Commanded Us to have Stewardship

for the Most Innocent Souls in the Universe.

Photo Credit

Monique Misfeldt

This is My Passion.

PREFACE

I am sure you have had a light bulb go off in your head and then said to yourself, "OMG, I have to do something about this!" One of those 'aha' moments that you just needed to share. A revelation that inspired you to act!

That's this book for me! As a holistic veterinarian, I have keenly observed relationships between my clients and their pets for over thirty years. I can attest to the often odd or at least surprising similarities between a pet and his guardian. I have been a witness to the positive or negative effect that a guardian has on a pet.

Do you think an anxious cat enthusiast simply purchases a neurotic feline by misfortune? Why would a diabetic dad have a son *and* two unrelated dogs, all of whom developed diabetes? How could a child develop vaccine-related fibrosarcoma and the family's Golden Retriever develop the same affliction? Is this just strange coincidence, or is there something more at work here?

When I sit on the floor with a pet and talk to the pet parent for much longer than the average vet, I learn a lot about the emotional and physical health of that pet parent. Something has guided me to embrace those experiences, learn more about human health care and to attempt to address the final piece of truly holistic pet care which is you!

My holistic journey has led me down paths with some difficult crossroads. My choices have led to enlightenment, and I think a better practice of medicine. Learning has been fun, satisfying and life changing!

This journey has caused me to reach a place of awakening. This new awareness will never allow me to go back to my former ways of thinking or practice. I am so grateful for where I am and looking forward to where I have been designed to go.

Decision making has become more difficult for me, as my opportunities are overwhelming. As you will see in Chapter 1 Conscious Language™, it is important that I say, "I choose to move forward with clarity!" I would like to share my thoughts and the applicable ramifications with you.

This book will surely impact the mind, body and spirit of you and your pets! Perhaps I will inspire you to have some 'aha' moments of your own!

I fondly recall the anecdotes described so vividly by Dr. James Herriot in his books, which I read as a teen. Now I have lived my own James Herriot life. Please join my journey.

Please pass this book on. Sharing posts on Facebook is great. But sharing a book is grand!

Introduction: Let's Talk!
Whiskey's Story

So, this new client, Joe, brings in his raw, bald, cat named Whiskey. She had been suffering from this horrific skin condition for more than a year. She was covered with crusty, red sores. The only place she had fur left was on her head where she could not reach to lick. Joe had taken Whiskey to several vets, including the state veterinary teaching hospital. She had been injected with long-acting antibiotics and long-acting steroids. She had even received some hormonal treatment. She had undergone a lot of testing, but no reason for her condition had been identified and no treatment had been successful. Joe was on the verge of requesting humane euthanasia because he could not stand to see Whiskey be so miserable any longer.

Once again, I was told that I was this pet's last resort. So, whatever I tried, we had nothing to lose!

I figured Whiskey was allergic to something and I thought that if I offered to take Whiskey out of her current home, I could remove her from a potential allergen as well as control her diet and her treatment. My first impulse was to bathe her because in some way I wanted to give her skin some immediate relief. I explained to Joe that I felt Whiskey would need what I call daily detox soaks. He was mystified at the idea of soaking his cat and so he was quick to take me up on the idea of keeping her in the clinic. He would miss her, but he was quite exhausted at the futility of her care.

My plan was to soak Whiskey every day in a soothing, coconut oil soap with essential oils. I demonstrated this procedure for Joe so that he wouldn't worry about Whiskey. I filled a new litter pan with warm water, the special soap and about 3 drops of lavender. I swaddled this apprehensive kitty snuggly in a large bath towel. I slowly lowered her into the water while cradling her in my arms. I could feel her relax as the warm water gradually penetrated the thick towel. Lavender is emotionally calming and is soothing to even irritated skin. My plan was to repeat this daily, add other oils to the protocol and to transition her to a raw meat diet.

Joe signed a release and was on his way. He came back weekly to visit. We began making good progress with Whiskey right away.

She had been eating a variety of dry kibble diets, even some "hypoallergenic" ones prescribed by previous veterinarians. Unfortunately, what they all had in common is starch. I have become a fanatic about removing starch from the carnivore diet. It is common sense to me that a feline should eat a species-appropriate, meat-based diet, free of excessive inflammatory carbohydrates.[1] Whiskey was a walking ball of inflammation! She was a middle-aged kitty, set in her ways, so it took some patience and persistence to convert her from the addictive, sugary dry kibble diet to canned meat and then to fresh, raw, balanced food. It is intuitive to me that rabbit as a food would be a go-to diet to prevent or repair many conditions in dogs and cats, and in fact, it is fabulous!

Whiskey improved every day. In a month, all her fur had regrown; she was a beautiful kitty! She loved us! She enjoyed every day at the "spa" with my staff who diligently implemented her care.

But I was concerned that after all this effort and hard work we might send Whiskey home only to have her condition recur. How could I know what had caused this devastating situation in the first place?
See Chapter 3 for the rest of the story!

Introduction: Purpose

I wrote this book to help guardians be better advocates for their pets. The more real a relationship feels the more compassion and understanding will be shared between the parties in that twosome, in this case, you and your pet! I believe today's feline and canine children have some desires which need to be heard and implemented. Today's pet parents want a deeper relationship with their pets and want to fulfill every need, if only they knew what those needs were!

In this book you will learn that what you say, what you think, what you feed, the veterinary care that you choose, the home you provide, and even your self-care has an impact on your pet!

Journey with me into the mind-body connection that controls your pet's emotional and physical well-being and then Live with Your Pet in Mind!

You will come to understand what natural nutrition is and why fresh, species appropriate food makes the most sense for your carnivorous feline or your omnivorous canine. You will gain the knowledge to make better informed choices regarding your pet's health care. You will gain awareness for how your home and environmental surroundings can impact your pet's quality of life and longevity. You will round out your holistic approach to pet health care by realizing that your emotional and physical health is an important part of this picture. It is important to your dog, and surprisingly to some perhaps, even your cat cares about you!

CHAPTER 1

What Are You Saying? *Conscious Language*™

Positive Thoughts Matter

"Our words are the quantum templates of health, abundance, peace and relationships! .... We have the power to alter what we experience. Today, modern scientists describe precisely the same irony. Using the language of quantum physics rather than poetry, a growing number of leading-edge scientists suggest that the universe, and everything in the universe, "is" what it "is" because of consciousness itself — the same consciousness that is affected by our words." [1]

Wow! That is deep! Sounds a bit new age, doesn't it? Well, if you really think about this, it is not a new theory. It is simply the recognition of what has been forever. Who is the original progenitor of this concept? Well, God of course! What did He say? "I am." And He was and is and always will be. He said, "Let there be light and there was. How is that possible? This is manifestation of conscious thought. This is the power of thought.

In my opinion, the study of quantum physics is man getting close to understanding God. Yet, the nature of God will always surpass all our understanding. The thirst for this knowledge began in the Garden of Eden and the quest continues today.

Conscious Thought

Why does this matter to an integrative veterinarian? This is vitally important because I believe if we could control our thoughts, we could control our health and that of our pets. Good thoughts-good health. Bad thoughts-bad health. I am not implying any level of simplicity here. This is complex, but as are many goals in life, it is often about the journey, not the destination. I learn from every thought I have, every word I speak and every sentence I write. I hope that my words will have a profound impact on you for your sake and that of your pet.

What does God have to do with it?

If God is so great, then why don't we just put our faith in Him and let nature take its course? Well, yes, honestly, that is what we should do; put our faith and trust in God, but recognize that is a *thought*. Your conscious mind must think it, so that your unconscious mind can believe it. What you think about most, you will believe. What you honestly believe, manifests. Has God ever told us that our thoughts matter and that we should control them for better outcomes? As a matter of fact, yes, yes, He has!

In Philippians 4:6-9, while in prison, God's disciple Paul wrote with divine inspiration, "…*let your requests be made known unto God. And the peace of God, which passeth all understanding, shall keep your hearts and minds through Christ Jesus…whatsoever things are true, whatsoever things are honest, whatsoever things are lovely, whatsoever things are of good report; if there be any virtue, and if there be any praise, **think** on these things. Those things, which ye have both learned, and received, and heard, and seen in me, do: and the God of peace shall be with you.*"

My Bible explains this further, "*What we put into our minds determines what comes out in our words and actions. Paul tells us to program our minds with thoughts that are true, honest, just, pure, lovely, of good report, virtuous and praiseworthy.*" [2]

Open Your Mind

Just as I opened my mind to the concepts of natural nutrition 25 years ago, I opened my mind to this idea that 'our thoughts will manifest', a bit more recently. When I allow those, who cross my path to enter into my life with new ideas, I generally can't get enough. I travel the country seeking more and more education. I love that now I can get an abundance of education sitting in my cozy chair in my home with my pets by my side and I don't have to travel as much! But I think there is something to be said for the social interactions during a large group learning experience. This is a good example.

Marcella's Highest Potential Academy

I found myself at a weekend seminar in Scottsdale, Arizona organized by Marcella Vonn Harting, founder of the Highest Potential Academy. There were a variety of excellent speakers. All were there with the intent to help us better ourselves. I am typically not a meditative person and certainly not into reciting mantras, but this was different. One incredibly wise and humorous presenter that weekend led us in the following repetitive mantra:

He said, "I love. I touch. I breathe. I stay. I feel."
Then he said, repeat, "I LOVE. I TOUCH. I BREATHE. I STAY. I FEEL."
Again, "I LOVE. I TOUCH. I BREATHE. I STAY. I FEEL."

Now, *believe*, "I qualify with grace and ease now and continuously."
Repeat: "I QUALIFY WITH GRACE AND EASE NOW AND CONTINUOUSLY." [3]

This mantra is an example of Conscious Language™. The wise man who led me, and the inquisitive group of leaders with whom I participated, was Robert Tennyson Stevens. He coined the phrase Conscious Language™. He is a word master! We in the audience were gripped by his usage of the English language! When you begin to understand the derivation of words, the importance of how you use these words begins to set in. Careful or Conscious Language™ becomes imperative. Pretty soon you are afraid to open your mouth because you know that saying something wrong can sabotage your life!

The unconscious mind will hear what you say and make bad decisions based on the misinformation. Your right brain's conscious language tells your left brain what is real.

Ponder for a moment this mind-blowing true story:

A schizophrenic woman was diabetic when she was personality A. She needed insulin and had to be careful how she ate. When this same woman was personality B, she was NOT diabetic; she did not need insulin. She did NOT BELIEVE that she was diabetic, so physically, she was not! [4]

Sound crazy? Remarkably interesting, I think! This lends credence to the assertion that what we *genuinely believe* will manifest.

The sooner you believe, the more deeply you believe, the more immediate the manifestation.

So, that mantra is very positive. Can you understand that if your thoughts become reality, then it is quite important to have positive thoughts?

A friend of mine always said, "You can't afford the power of a negative thought." I think she was quoting a motivational speaker. She was quite positive and lived quite a successful life in her own regard, which is what matters most, of course!

Negative Thoughts Matter

Let's look at the flip side of this then. What if you are having negative thoughts? Whether you are angry with yourself, a family member or with your pet, many dogs and cats sense this and take it to heart. Suppressed emotions can cause disease. Oriental medial philosophy often explains a common Chinese diagnosis, liver qi stagnation in this way. Liver Qi Stagnation is one of the most common imbalances diagnosed in our Western culture. The Liver controls the smooth flow of Qi throughout the body which is crucial to the health of all of the organ systems of the body.

This is why symptoms of **liver qi stagnation** seem so varied. Signs may include:
Anger, irritability, and frustration
Feeling stuck emotionally
Depression
Anxiety, stress easily
Tenderness around ribs
Pain on the sides
Hard to swallow-lump in throat
Sigh often
PMS
IBS

What if you are always saying, "I want this, I want that"? Even this is a negative thought. Wanting is admitting that there is a lack. This is not a positive thought. Noticing and expressing the negatives of a situation only help that situation to continue to be so.

Worry vs. Concern

Are you a worrier? Do you worry about yourself, about your pet? Isn't that okay, perhaps even a virtue? Isn't it nice to be concerned about others? Concern and worry are not the same. Here again God's guidance comes in handy!

In Matthew 6:25–34, my Bible lists seven reasons *not* to worry:

1) *The same God who created life in you can be trusted with the details of your life.*
2) *Worrying about the future hampers your efforts for today.*
3) *Worrying is more harmful than helpful.*
4) *God does not ignore those who depend on Him.*
5) *Worrying shows a lack of faith in and understanding of God.*
6) *Worrying keeps us from the real challenges God wants us to pursue!*
7) *Living one day at a time keeps us from being consumed with worry.*

This Bible study guide goes on to explain the difference between worry and genuine concern, *"Worry immobilizes, but concern moves you to action!"*[2]

In my experience, the pet guardians who *worry* most about their pets, frequently, have chronically ill pets. Those with *concern* are mobilized to action and the pair: pet and parent, live quality lives together, regardless of longevity.

Molly's Story

Five years ago, I was taking care of a poodle patient whose mom died. The dad was undoubtedly distraught by this loss and when the dog began defecating and urinating in the home, Mr. Owner had no patience. He brought this pet in for me to "fix her". After I explained that we needed to do some tests to find out what might be wrong, he said, "She's crapping and peeing all over, can't you give her a pill?" I said I would call him with test results, and we would have to go from there. Her blood work showed an elevated alkaline phosphatase. This can correlate with Cushing's disease, as well as her symptoms of excessive thirst, excessive urine volume and poor hair coat. She was bald!

I informed Mr. Owner that his little dog, Molly, needed a low dose dexamethasone suppression test. I told him to let us know when he would like to schedule that.

Shortly thereafter, my office received a call from the local humane society inquiring as to Molly's vaccine status. She had been relinquished to their custody. This abandonment of Molly was particularly sad because she had lost her female guardian not too long ago. I have found that many Cushing's patients have suffered some significant emotional trauma prior to the onset of this diagnosis.

I asked the humane personnel if she could give Molly to us to work on her health and then we could try to place her for adoption. She was happy to agree to this, as at their facility, Molly would likely have been euthanized. Most people don't like to adopt dogs with such significant problems.

We completed Molly's testing, confirmed her diagnosis and began a natural course of treatment. Cushings is also called hyperadrenocorticism. The adrenal glands overproduce cortisol, the body's stress hormone. This causes the symptoms which Molly exhibited.

During this time, Molly had a conversation with Rebecca, the animal communicator, who said, "Molly feels that her fur is a burden." This was sad. Molly was living in the reception area of my clinic and clients commonly inquired as to what was wrong with her coat. She had no hair! Obviously, this made Molly self-conscious.

Additionally, Molly asked Rebecca if I could be her mom. Molly had terrible separation anxiety. As we developed some structure in her life, Molly began trusting that when I left her sight, indeed I would return. Molly moved into my house. Molly's anxiety diminished. So, yes, she is still my dog and now, when I leave, she sleeps on the chair and no longer cries and scratches on the door. She also has a nice coat of white curls!

Molly continues to be my most difficult pet challenge. The universe put Molly into my life. She adds an element of stress to my days, but her interactions with me are a constant reminder to me to strive for positive thoughts and positive, careful, Conscious Language™. If good deeds could get me there, Molly would be my ticket to Heaven! On the days when I lose my patience with her, she is my elevator ride south.

Frequently, I need to apologize to Molly and to myself for my negative thoughts or negative Conscious Language™. If I say, or worse yet, believe, that Molly is an exasperating dog, then she will continue to be so. You may have a similar situation with a pet or a family member. For the good of all, put a positive spin on it!

Good Conscious Language™ is the key to your success in all areas of your emotional, physical, and spiritual life!

CHAPTER 2

What Are You Thinking? *Telepathy*

Photo Courtesy Melody Carranza

My Telepathic Dog

Mork was my soul dog. I sure do miss him. He was my little man. After we lost Marty, our beautiful, perfect, Golden Retriever, Mork initially seemed quite a misfit, some kind of Corgi/Cairn Terrier mix I think, but when people asked, I said he was a "Russian Wirehair". This made him feel uniquely special. I wouldn't let the groomer mess with his crazy hair do. It was his trademark.

Mork was one of those guys that could not get enough fetch. I could throw that ball far into the field 100 times and every time, he would bring it back. Drop it and stare at me saying, "Throw the ball, throw the ball, throw the ball; dang it, throw the ball!" His little tail stub wiggling. Periodically, he would drop the ball five feet in front of me so that I would have to get up out of my lawn chair to throw it, now who was doing the fetching? If I said, "Bring it!" He would give the ball a little nudge with his nose, as if to say, "Is that close enough for you? Now, get up woman and throw that ball!" It didn't matter how hot out it was; he kept demanding more ball play, even when his mouth was dripping with saliva.
Of course, like a mother who must pull her kid out of a chilling swimming pool when his lips are blue, but he still wants to stay in, I had to be the one to discontinue Mork's fetching game.

As soon as the thought entered my head that this would be my last throw and then we would go in the house, guess what? He was not bringing that ball back!

Did he know what I was thinking? Sure enough! Time and again this would happen! I had to make a conscious effort to try to control my thoughts and trick him into bringing that ball back after that last throw. Believe me, there were a lot of balls left out in the hay field! Many of them even got chopped up by the hay mower.

It was always a fun quest to buy a new ball for Mork whenever I traveled. It gave me a great excuse to check out natural pet retailers in many communities across the country and then pack his new ball in my luggage to surprise him when I got home. And, yes, when I walked in the door, he seemed to know I had something for him and was anxious to have me unpack!

Mork and I did not need to verbalize in order to know what the other was thinking, this was our telepathy. Was it real?

What do you do when you want to learn more about something? I write about it.

Did you ever notice that kids who love animals become vets, your college friends who were on drugs became pharmacists, people who like to argue become attorneys and individuals with emotional problems become psychiatrists?

I think people gravitate towards a field they need to know more about to help themselves. I often choose a topic of interest to write about, NOT because I am an expert on that topic, but because I want to learn more about it, because I think it might be useful to me. Then, when I understand it, it is natural for me, and I think for other humans as well, to want to share that knowledge with others. I was certainly a telepathy skeptic, always looking for the trick, asking, how could they know that? But I was intrigued. I had to keep an open mind and learn more.

Famous Jaytee Telepathy Experiment[1]

I watched a short Gallivant film produced with the cooperation of Rupert Sheldrake, Pam Smart and the Science Unit of ORF, Vienna. They set up an experiment to test the telepathic abilities of a dog; Pam's dog, Jaytee. In the UK documentary, furry little Jaytee is left home with the grandparents while his mum goes for tea with a friend. A spy cam is put in the house to watch Jaytee's behavior. The camera's timer is synchronized with a camera which follows the day trip of Jaytee's mum.

As you watch the film you can see the clock roll forward in time, while little Jaytee lies at Grandma's feet for several hours. (Pam and her parents have no knowledge of when she intends to head home.) Jaytee's mum bustles around town with her friend, shopping, and drinking tea. Heading home would not be at any normal, routine time. In fact, she would head home in a taxi so that the sound of her usual vehicle would not become a part of this experiment.

As you see Jaytee's mum tell her friend she will be going now and get into a taxi, you simultaneously, on the adjacent screen, witness Jaytee get up and head to the window at precisely the same time, and sit there patiently waiting her arrival.

The family had witnessed this behavior many times themselves.
But the synchronizing of the cameras demonstrated that at the exact time mum *thought* about coming home, Jaytee perceived her thought and went to the window to watch for her.

Based on this and many other stories, Rupert Sheldrake wrote a book called, "Dogs That Know When Their Owners Are Coming Home: And Other Unexplained Powers of Animals".

I am convinced that animals are telepathic, but are we? This is controversial.

Telepathy: Fake or Fact?

I watched Sylvia Browne on The Montel Williams Show, she performed supposed feats ranging from ghost detecting to offering details about missing persons and murder cases. Wow! Pretty impressive! Of course, the episode I remember best included a cat in her reading.

I recall three ladies together at the show, raised a hand and stood up next to Sylvia. They wanted to know about family members who had passed on. (This peek into the afterlife still particularly bothers me on many levels, but it is fascinating.) Sylvia said she could see or feel some things about the relatives, and then she said, "Who has the calico cat?" This brought one of the women to tears because her aunt had a calico cat. She felt this validated Sylvia's reading and made her believe that her dead aunt was doing well with her beloved cat at her side! Doesn't this stuff just freak you out?

I can handle the idea of telepathic communication among the living a bit better. Simply put by Wikipedia: Telepathy is the purported transmission of information from one person to another without using any of our known sensory channels or physical interaction. The term was coined in 1882 by a scholar of psychic research. He developed the term from tele meaning "distant" and pathos meaning "perception".[2]

Today, scientists still say telepathic communication between humans is not possible. Yet, they have designed equipment which can transfer thoughts electronically long distance from one person's brain to another's![3] Is this necessary? Or do we just need to tap into our innate ability? Do we just need to believe what many others already seem to know? After all, we are animals too.

CHAPTER 3

Stories of Animal Communication

The you label holistic  longer yourself a

practitioner, the kookier things will cross your path. During your journey of open mindedness, many of those kooky things become not so kooky anymore. My exposure to Animal Communication certainly fits this category.

By Animal Communication, I do not mean how two or more animals communicate with each other. Volumes have been written about that. I remember growing up in 4-H horse project, attending project meetings and learning how a horse will pin back her ears and without a word, drive another horse away from a hay pile. That's subtle!

I'm not talking about communication with your pet by observing body language either, although this is very important! Dr. Karen Becker wrote a great article called, "Seven Tips to Read Your Dog's Body Language". Trainers and behaviorists have been observing these cues to facilitate their craft and service to pet guardians for eons.

Interspecies Communication

I am talking about Animal Communicators who use their God-given gift to "hear" or envision what a pet is thinking or saying. Believing that this is possible is a stretch for many. Believe me, I was a huge skeptic, and I still believe there are charlatans in this arena. However, when you see the real thing and you are taught by a genuine master, you can understand how this is possible and believe that it is a real talent.

As my holistic minded clients became more trusting of me, they opened up and often told me what had brought them there that day. Often it was not an obvious symptom or a wound, nor an annual checkup. Rather, it was upon the advice of the Animal Communicator who had had a conversation with their pet.

Charlie's Story

One client's story went like this: "A friend of mine suggested I take my cats to an Animal Communicator for fun. I thought, okay, it's not that expensive, I'll try it. Well, now I am concerned because Charlie told her that he has a mass pressing on his bladder. He seems okay, but doc, can you check this out?"

So, I did. I thought this was ridiculous to expose this poor cat to x-rays, but we took a radiograph any way and I did see a suspicious increased opacity adjacent to the bladder! Well, radiographs can be a bit subjective. So, I told the client that if she really wanted to be sure and for possible surgical planning, we should do an abdominal ultrasound. So, I had a specialist perform this procedure. Sure enough, a mass was present!

Well, I needed to learn more about this Animal Communication thing!

Who was this Animal Communicator and how does she do what she does? If I were going to affirm her findings and if I were going to consider referring others to her, I needed to know more. I invited her to my practice to speak to a few test animals'.

What Happened to Whiskey?

Remember Whiskey from the Let's Talk Introduction?
So, what had caused Whiskey's devastating situation in the first place? If only she could tell us, right?
Well, I found out Rebecca could!

Rebecca was an Animal Communicator who visited my practice periodically. I was usually busy seeing patients and didn't have time to pay much attention to what she was doing. I did take some of my own pets to her initially because I wanted to make sure that I did not let a total whack job loose on my clientele. I was skeptical, but I promised myself I would always remain cautious, but open minded to new holistic modalities, as I had been frequently surprised by what clients reported to me to be beneficial to their pets.

This day, I asked Rebecca if she had time to talk to Whiskey. We went into my cozy little acupuncture room with its special oriental lanterns, meditative music, paw print blankets and well-used pillows on the floor. Whiskey walked around the space like she owned it. She had been with us for quite some time, so she had no fear. I told Rebecca Whiskey's name and I said that I would like to know if Whiskey knew what was bothering her. Rebecca closed her eyes and thought for moment. She said Whiskey does not like the white powder that the woman puts in the carpet. It makes her burn. Holy cow!

I did not know there was a "woman". Only Joe had ever stopped in all this time. I am not one to pry, so I did not know if he had a girlfriend or a wife. Whiskey seemed to want to tell Rebecca a bit more about this woman. Now, keep in mind that often an animal communicator will say that a pet "says" something, but in reality, the communicator gets a feeling or sees a picture and then describes it in the pet's tone or voice. Whiskey said, "I think the lady likes the brown dog better than me and that makes me feel bad." What was up with that? I had to ask Joe next time he was in!

I'm thinking, wow, that's mean. Did she tell Joe that she likes the dog more than Whiskey? How devastating! I wanted to tell her, "Don't say that in front of your cat"!
So, the next time Joe stopped in to visit Whiskey I had to explain that I had taken her to an animal communicator and that I think we had learned why she developed a skin condition. I was excited, but also apprehensive. Sure enough, Joe did have a wife and you are not going to believe this, but yes, she did use carpet powder! I was on a roll! Next, I told him that Whiskey thought his wife liked their dog more than her. Oh boy, Joe said, "We don't have a dog." I was momentarily deflated.

I explained that Rebecca often sees pictures that are telepathically sent to her by the pet. Whiskey showed Rebecca a picture of a brown dog. Is there another dog in the family or neighborhood? Joe said, "Oh my, gosh, my wife shoos Whiskey away from a brown dachshund statue she keeps up high on a shelf! She is afraid that Whiskey will break it. The dog statue is a family heirloom!"

Goose bumps!

Animal Communication Explained by Rebecca

I took one of Rebecca's communication courses. I loved the way she explained the idea of animal communication. She did not try to make it seem mysterious. She did not try to make it seem that she was unique for having this gift, although those who knew her felt she was *incredibly special*. She was matter of fact in her explanation which went like this:

"Animal Communication, also known as interspecies telepathic communication is the ability to telepathically connect with a being of another species and communicate with them. Two-way communication is accomplished not only with words, but with images, feelings, thoughts, and emotions.

All species are born with this ability. Unfortunately for humans, telepathic abilities are quickly lost, not only because we become so accustomed to verbal speech, but also because our society does not readily accept this form of communication.

Some people may think animal communication is very odd, or even unbelievable. The truth is that by communicating with other species, one begins to understand the interconnection of all living things. One can experience the beauty and harmony that is possible when we understand that all living creatures are intelligent beings, with their own feelings, thoughts, desires and perceptions of life and those they interact with.

Having the opportunity to find out what your animal companion's thoughts, feelings and attitudes are, can greatly enhance your relationship with one another and bring great joy and happiness into your life."

Rebecca shared some great examples of this. I remember her explaining this interaction between mom and son. A little boy sat at the breakfast table watching the birds outside the window. He said, "Mommy, the birdies say they want some seeds." Mommy answered, "Oh, honey, the birdies can't talk." The little boy felt foolish and stopped telling his mommy what he heard the animals say. As he got older, he believed the things he heard were just thoughts and let it go. Pretty soon he didn't hear the animals at all anymore.

Have you ever been sitting at your laptop, typing away, and then just stopped, looked at the dog's water bowl and said, "Do you need some fresh water? Let me get some for you." You got up, emptied, and refilled the bowl and then went back to your business thinking that that was your idea. Really, the dog just let you know he needed that.

The amazing "reading" of Whiskey's mind was by no means an isolated incident in my experiences with communicators and the interactions culminating with medically verifiable outcomes.

Leonard's Story

James is one of my most particular clients. He was always concerned about his cats and how they felt. He did not want them to ever be uncomfortable. When one cat developed a diseased tooth, instead of extraction, he opted for a root canal with a veterinary dental specialist. James was excited to learn that there was a woman who could let him know if his cats felt well emotionally and physically, and if they had any desires that he should be aware of to make their lives even better.

James is a highly intelligent man and noticeably quiet. He simply shared the names of his cats, Leonard, Sam, and Buster, with the communicator and then let her do her magic. Rebecca sits or stands with her eyes closed and sometimes puts her hands over her face to get focused and concentrate. Some communicators can make a connection over the phone.

Without touching, in this case, communicator Carolee Biddle either saw or "felt" an area that was warm in the center of Leonard's back. She told James he might want to have a vet examine Leonard. Leonard was not lame, and James had provided no history of a problem for the communicator. Leonard had come to me for annual exams, and I had not diagnosed any problems with his spine. James wanted to know if there was any truth to this concern raised by Carolee.

We took a lateral spine radiograph of Leonard and found two mid spine vertebrae fused together! Goose bumps! I had never seen this anomaly in a cat.

Much to my surprise, this surely validated the telepathic communication. Carolee was trained by Rebecca and inherited Rebecca's donkeys after her passing and lovingly cares for them to this day. Many have had beautiful experiences with Rebecca and have learned from her how to enhance their God-given gift.

Testimonials for Rebecca

With permission, I am sharing the following beautiful testimonial with you by Becky Stritt from Lake Geneva, Wisconsin. She reiterates from her own experience, many of the comments which I have made so far regarding Rebecca's talent. You will see why I believe that the mind connection that you have with your pet can go ever deeper and can have such a profound impact on the emotional and physical health for you both.

Praises Written at Kindred Spirits[1]

After doing months of research on animal communication, I actively sought out a communicator. Luckily for me and my dog- I found Rebecca Moravec. I contacted her with a few questions about the process and she made me so at ease with her kind and gentle manner, I knew I had to have a reading with her and my Old English sheepdog, Millie.

One of my main reasons for wanting to do this was that Millie was constantly sick. Also, I felt that Millie and I just weren't bonding like I had hoped we would. During my first reading with Rebecca, she immediately hit on Millie's constant nausea. She told me exactly what was making Millie sick- which I changed and saw a 100% difference overnight.

I had battled for months trying to fix this problem for Millie and Rebecca brought us the instant answer. I was (and still am) amazed. This is just one of the many things she has uncovered in her readings with Millie. She has also helped me conquer behavior and training issues, as well as just helping me to know Millie's very comical, very loving personality.

Since then, I have had 3 more readings, and also attended Rebecca's Basic Animal Communication Workshop. I guess the best way I could describe these experiences is life changing. Rebecca has a gift that I just wish everyone could experience. Not only are her readings amazing, but her personality also makes you so comfortable. She has helped me tremendously, taking my relationship with Millie to a level that is more than I ever knew it could be. I see my dog in a different light now- Rebecca has helped me see Millie's true personality, which has been fun as well as so helpful. Rebecca has also shown me how to open my heart and mind and enjoy the utterly amazing gift she offers. I know that anyone who meets Rebecca, and experiences her gifts through her work, will be so glad they did. - **Becky Stritt, Lake Geneva, WI**

Praises for Rebecca from Animal Doctor Clients

I met Rebecca Moravec through my vet, Dr. Jodie. I was having some issues connecting to my cat, Bob. I had adopted him from Animal Doctor when he was about one year old and was told he had a rough start in life. He was a nervous and tentative guy. After several months, I was still not able to get near him. He did develop a friendship with my one-year-old standard poodle, Penny. Dr. Jodie suggested I make an appointment with Rebecca to find out what Bob needed. When I spoke to Rebecca, she relayed Bob's thoughts to me. He felt I moved too fast, and that Penny seemed to block him from allowing me to approach him. I made a few simple changes. I taught Penny to respect "Bob time and space". I moved slower. After ten minutes, I was petting Bob! Our relationship continued to improve. I could not have done this without Rebecca sharing her gift.

Over the years, each conversation Rebecca had with my animals provided new insights which strengthened our relationships.

In one conversation, Penny complained to Rebecca of back pain near her tail. I had not noticed anything in Penny's movements that would have led me to think she was in pain. But I took Rebecca's gift seriously and I made an appointment with Dr. Jodie. A radiograph of Penny's spine revealed a diagnosis of spondylosis! Dr. Jodie prescribed an herb to help her.

Animal Communication Helps with Making End of Life Decisions.

Penny's mom went on to explain that late in life, Penny developed serious liver disease…

I came home from work and Penny looked like she felt bad, near death kind of bad. I thought this was the end and it was time to put her to sleep. I called Rebecca to double check. Rebecca connected with Penny. Penny didn't want to die. She needed more time. So, I listened. I continued regular vet appointments and eastern supplements and western meds recommended by Dr. Jodie. I talked with Penny through Rebecca every three to four months. I cherished every moment I had with Penny.

Penny's mom believed this was an extended gift of time due to the collaboration of an integrative veterinarian and an animal communicator.

It was through Rebecca that I heard Penny's voice and understood what she needed emotionally and physically. Because of Rebecca's gift I did not put her to sleep on that day. We had 14 more months together! When I thought it was time to say goodbye, I called Rebecca just to be sure it was what Penny wanted, and to say goodbye. Rebecca relayed my thoughts, love and goodbyes to Penny, who was lying on the floor next to me. Rebecca told me Penny was ready to be in Heaven and was separating from me.

As she said this to me on the phone, Penny rose, moved a few feet from me and laid down again. I called Dr. Jodie who met me at the clinic. Thanks to Dr. Jodie, Penny passed gracefully, and with dignity moved on to Heaven.

I am blessed to have known Rebecca. Due to her gift, I was better able to provide my pets the life that made them happy. I am blessed to know Dr. Jodie. Through her gifts of intuition, belief in telepathic gifts, and knowledge of eastern and western medicine, my animals live healthy lives.

*I have many more stories about my experiences with Rebecca and her gifts. About how she was able to connect with my animals and relay information only my pets would know. I have even taken some classes she taught. Rebecca touched my life and my pets' lives in beautiful ways. I will be forever grateful to her that she had the courage to share her gifts with me and countless others. She will be eternally missed!—**Wendy Fisenne, Muskego, Wi.***

Animal Communication Can End Behavioral Problems

Pet Personalities Shine Through!

My cat, Frodo, had been scratching at doors all throughout the night, every night, for at least four months! He would scratch incessantly at closet doors, the bathroom door if it was shut, but mainly he would scratch at my computer room that housed one of my other cats, Mama Kitty. Frodo would scratch and paw excessively to no end, all night, no matter what I tried. I tried double sticky tape on the doors; I sprayed him with water, placed motion detector air sprayers, blocked the door with a gate, whatever I could think of! Every night would end the same, hours of battle with him, only to end with me locking him downstairs.

When I finally took Frodo to see Rebecca she confirmed his name, and then connected with him to communicate. The first thing she said was, "He does not like closed doors". To which I replied, "That is why I am here!" She continued to tell me that there was one door in particular he wanted to get into. He thought it was a "fun" room. Not only did the room contain my desk and computer, but all my crafting supplies as well-lots of fun for a cat! He also said that he really wanted to play with the cat that lived in the room. Rebecca asked me why he couldn't go in there so she could explain it to him. I said that Mama Kitty was an older, shy cat that did not like other cats and therefore she lived in that room. It was her sanctuary and she loved it. I also had many crafting items that Mama Kitty never bothered, but Frodo would likely play with. Rebecca asked me what Frodo's "punishment" would be if he scratched at the door. I told her the only thing that worked was locking him downstairs, which meant another locked door. Frodo didn't understand why Mama Kitty did not want to play with him and he did not like being locked downstairs. After telling Rebecca what my solutions were she communicated to Frodo saying that if he continued to scratch at the door he would be locked downstairs and that whenever I would go into the room he could come with me. He was not allowed to bother Mama Kitty but he could come in the room to play. That night he did not scratch at the door for the first night in over four months. He has never scratched at the door since! Mama Kitty has since become braver. She moved into the living area where Frodo will try to play with her, but she is brave enough now to swat at him to say no. That door still remains closed all the time unless I am in it. I no sooner turn the doorknob and he runs into the room, every single time... He loves to follow me in there. He will touch just about everything he can, or is allowed, maybe sit on my lap or the bed, or once he is satisfied, he leaves. I am so grateful I was able to have Rebecca communicate with Frodo because I am sure he would have never stopped!

From Rebecca, I learned that my little black cat, Berlioz can be very funny. Rebecca's communications were very true to his nature and behavior. I had just decided to adopt Seymore, a large, orange cat from the outdoors, and Berlioz did not like that idea! As soon as Rebecca started to communicate Berlioz said, "I don't want any more cats to come into the house." Rebecca said that Berlioz believed the new cat to be "rude, smelly, and walked in like he owned the place". Seymore definitely did smell! I had applied *essential oils to most of the cats bedding to help with the adjustment. Seymore had tried out every bed and was very much a tomcat! He had walked right into our house like he had lived there his whole life! He never had any issues adjusting. As far as being rude, Berlioz has very high standards, I guess! He eventually accepted Seymore. Berlioz also told Rebecca that there was a toy that he especially liked, a blue ball with a feather on it. It seemed to move by itself and that intrigued him. Two weeks prior I had purchased a battery operated blue ball with a feather on it!—**Nancy Rusnak, CVT, Kenosha, Wi.***

Goose bumps!

You can understand why the passing of Rebecca is such a loss for the animal-loving community, but she left those of us whom she touched with such valuable insight!

Pets Mirror Us

On the flip side, what can our own personal little kindred spirits tell us about our own health? Remember how my Mork expressed his concern for my busy schedule? I believe if given the opportunity, our pets will warn us, try to change us for the better, and even take on our problems.

Diamo's Story

A fourth-year veterinary student, Jodie Joseph, wrote about her internship experience at Holistic Pet Care in New Jersey. She shared with readers about a Siamese patient, Diamo who helped his guardian, Darlene survive cancer by sharing it with her! Both pet and parent had cancer, and both survived! Both went into remission the same week! Darlene had serious metastatic breast cancer.

Ms. Joseph explains more about this remarkable story, *"Darlene knew exactly where all forty tumors were because Diamo had pointed them out, nudging each area... However, there was one spot Diamo did not identify, her pancreas. Darlene had metastatic breast cancer to basically every organ except her pancreas. I believe Diamo took that on because it is a death sentence in human medicine. I believe they fought the cancer together for themselves and for each other. Although Diamo passed (four years later due to kidney failure), Darlene is very much alive and in remission. She has a new cat, Piccolino, from the same breeder who is her new protector."*

I have found it to be quite interesting how often a pet is found to have a disorder very similar to the guardian or another family member. Is your pet a sponge or a canary in the coal mine? Will your pet take on a problem with you or become ill before you in order to alert you? Does this happen because of the kindred spirit mind interaction? Does this happen because what you believe manifests? Does this happen because you both eat similarly or live under the same roof?

It is a bit unnerving to learn that pet and parent have similar disorders. It is also difficult to decide how much to share when I believe a pet parent's thoughts or behaviors are causing the pet's illness, or worse, caused the pet's passing.

I have rarely been sadder or upset than when I have to tell a pet parent that my patient, their pet, has lung cancer due to second or third hand smoke. Read more on this in Chapter 7.

CHAPTER 4

What 4 Things Does Your Pet Want?

Is your pet a   positive
thinker? I believe my pets have been quite successful in
choosing to manifest their wants or needs! Animal
communicators have helped us to recognize common pet
desires. I am sure your intuition or telepathy has helped you
provide for your pet's demands.

Four of the Most Commonly Mentioned Pet Desires

- ❁ **Yummy Food**
- ❁ **Cozy Bed**
- ❁ **Good Vet**
- ❁ **Loving Guardian**

❀ Yummy Food

Animal communicators have told me that in almost every discussion they have with a pet, the dog or cat talks about food. They want good food. They want yummy food. They want to try what you're eating! My grand doggy told Rebecca that he wanted some of my son-in-law's pizza. He had never had any. Now, do you think they feel guilty when eating pizza in front of him? You bet! So, yes, that little stinker gets a nibble of pizza now and then.

So, is that okay? Many of us were told by our parents, "Never feed the dog from your plate. Never allow the cat to eat on the counter. Don't share your food or they will beg, and your food is not good for them." Is that true? What is meant by "their food" any way? And is it good for them? Years ago, it was normal to feed scraps to the pets, the dog outside the bones, the cat in the barn, some milk. When did a dry kibble diet become *pet* food? If in nature the average cat consumes a mouse per day, what nutrition is in a mouse, and shouldn't we mimic that when we feed our beloved companions? I will discuss this further in Chapter 5.

❀ Cozy Bed

Once, I married a guy who had six cats. That is partly what attracted me to him. But I had that beat! I had seven cats! Put that together and we had the Brady Bunch of the cat world. My ex told me that these cats needed their own comfortable accommodations to be content. He said, "Cats want a lot of beds!" I am telling you that helped so much to keep the peace in that multi-cat household!

Behavioral issues are a common reason for pet relinquishment to humane societies and shelters.

In my experience, cancer is on the rise. I believe environmental provisions can positively or negatively impact these two major problems. As a holistic veterinarian, I strive to identify and change causes of conditions which lead to poor quality of pet life or premature euthanasia.

What other home and environmental surroundings are important to your pet's well-being and what can YOU do to improve your pet's behavior, quality of life and increase longevity by enhancing his or her accommodations? Let's talk about that some more in Chapter 6.

❧ Good Vet

Children, pets, even adults don't generally like to go to the doctor. Why is that? Aren't doctors supposed to help you? Why wouldn't you want to go there? If you sit outside most veterinary clinics, you will see a dog trotting around outside beside his guardian, as he nears the door, his paws become brakes and the leash becomes a dragging instrument. If you could hear him screaming inside, he would be saying, "No mom, no, please, don't make me go in there!"

Well, gee, that's sad. Veterinarians and veterinary technicians, heck, even veterinary clinic receptionists go into the field because they love animals. It's sad to think their patients don't want to come through the door. What has transpired to make that so?

Let's see from the patient's perspective: You waited in a smelly, fear-filled, overcrowded reception area. You were dragged down the hallway and placed on a flat machine that you do not understand. Next, you waited in a tiny claustrophobic space only to have an odd smelling, white coated individual rush in with a handful of papers and odd tools wrapped around their neck. You could feel mom's nervousness, so you knew something was wrong. Next you were hoisted up onto a cold, stainless steel, slippery table. Someone wrapped you in a headlock. The white coat grabs your muzzle, pries open your mouth, shoves a plastic tube in your ears, puts a cold probe on your chest, squeezes your belly and perhaps even puts on a glove and shoves a finger up your butt! Next you felt the stab of a needle and a burn under your skin. To make matters worse, you were taken to the "back room" where no one told you what was going on. You had more stabbings in your neck and leg, tape that was sticky and pulled on your fur. You were really getting frustrated with the headlock routine around your neck. But, before you knew it, you woke up in a cage, disoriented, nauseous and with pain where some body parts used to be.

Let's examine how this experience could be very different with a holistic veterinarian in Chapter 6.

❧ Loving Guardian

Pets who have loving guardians do best. Pets need kind and healthy guardians. February 2015 Pet Statistics from the ASPCA show that approximately 2.7 million dogs and cats are killed every year because shelters are too full and there aren't enough adoptive homes. These cats and dogs may have been abused, abandoned, or relinquished.[1] Excess cats and dogs may have been bred in puppy mills, contributing to their overpopulation!

Who abuses animals?

Cruelty and neglect cross all social and economic boundaries and media reports suggest that animal abuse is common in both rural and urban areas.[2]

Intentional Cruelty

Sick people are often unkind to animals. Intentional cruelty to animals is correlated with other crimes including violence against people.[2] One of my saddest and happiest days in the office was when I met Peanut.

Peanut's Story

Peanut was adopted from Egypt! It was quite a feat for her new pet mommy to transport her overseas. Why was it so important to Peanut's new mom to go through all this effort just for a dog? Peanut had been used as a live piñata. She had been hung by hooks and beat with a wooden bat. She had multiple fractures in multiple legs. When I met her, I sat on the floor and she immediately crawled into my lap. No fear. Just trust and love. How could she have survived and how could she feel this way? How could anyone, and I think children, treat any living creature this way? Thankfully, a kind soul was able to intervene. Peanut received veterinary care. When we met, she was crippled, but ambulatory. We invited Peanut and her mom to participate in our iPAW pet fashion show. Together they proudly walked the runway, adorned in beautiful matching dresses. Peanut was revered as a symbol of strength and courage. Now Peanut has the ultimate loving guardian, just what she always wanted!

Hoarding

Many pet lovers are trying to do the right thing, but fall victim themselves and the animals they collect, to a hoarding situation. In this situation, the guardians need emotional and physical assistance. According to the Humane Society of the United States, *"those who intentionally abuse animals are predominantly men under 30, while those involved in animal hoarding are more likely to be women over 60."* The animals whose abuse is most often reported are dogs, cats, horses, and livestock. Based on the 1,423 U.S. cruelty cases on pet-abuse.com's 2011 digest in which species of the victim was specified: 70.1% involved dogs, 20.9% involved cats, and 24.1% involved other animals.[2]

Pets Given Away

In December 2015, an American Society for the Prevention of Cruelty to Animals® (ASPCA) survey found that 1 million households are re-homing their pets each year.

According to this study, *"the most common primary reasons for re-homing a pet were related to the pets themselves (46%), followed by family situations (27%) and housing issues (18%).*
Among the 46% who responded that they gave up a pet due to a pet-related issue, 26% said they could not afford medical care for their pets' health problems."[3]

Other specific reasons included a need for financial help with training or behavior, pet-friendly housing, free or low-cost spay/neuter services, pet food, temporary pet care or boarding, assistance in paying pet deposits for housing, landlord issues, and family member allergies.[3]

 I would add that in some situations when an owner can't afford veterinary care, it is because the difficulty in care or the financial commitment is not a priority and unfortunately some pets are still considered disposable commodities. I found it interesting that in this survey, 14% of those re-homed were taken in by a veterinarian.[3]

My veterinary practice, in conjunction with my non-profit, iPAW, has accepted ownership, repaired, or rehabilitated and then placed in adoptive homes hundreds of animals during the course of my career. We did not seek out these animals and we do not officially have a shelter. This service developed out of necessity and the desire to avoid unwarranted euthanasia.

Break the Cycle via Education and Self-Care

To break this cycle, it is important that we educate pet lovers so that they make good pet selection choices and so that they provide proper physical and emotional care for that pet.
The skills of an animal behaviorist are commonly sought to correct behaviors seen in pets who are adopted. Sometimes humans need help with their behavior and their role as half of a good relationship.

As in any relationship, you can't be there for your companion if you aren't taking good care of yourself. Our world is filled with an abundance of stressed-out humans! Our minds and bodies are unkempt due to overwork and poor nutrition.
Many people are looking for love and companionship.
You might seek love and companionship in a pet companion. It can be emotionally devastating to you and to your pet if your relationship doesn't work.
Your heart will break if it is wonderful but ends prematurely due to poor emotional or physical health. The initiation of your pet/pet parent relationship, and the nurturing of it, can be enhanced or sabotaged depending on your emotional stability and physical health.

I had a great experience when I used the talents of an animal communicator to help with a pet placement...

Iris' Story

Iris was a young, pudgy black cat with a timid demeanor. She was brought into my veterinary practice by a gentleman who had found her inside the underbelly of his car. We scanned her for a microchip; she had none. He needed to leave to get to work, so as often happens in a veterinary clinic, we suddenly had another cat. We had already agreed to provide refuge for some other kitties with the hope to cure what ailed them and then adopt them out, but sometimes that doesn't happen fast!

The presence of other cats made Iris nervous. She was not comfortable mingling with the rest of the group, so we provided a segregated litter pan, cozy bed, and water bowl in the doctor's office and closed the door. We would give her privacy for a bit until she came out of her shell.

We were not new to this idea of acclimation and then encouragement to assimilate. However, Iris was not having it. Days passed. We told her that she could leave the office. We coaxed her with food and treats to progressively move toward the front of the clinic. We told her she needed to be more outgoing and friendly if she wanted to meet people and find a new home. Most cats become inquisitive; at least at night they will come out and explore. Not Iris. She sat in that office window, staring, eating, and becoming fat.

Clients did not know she existed. If we carried her to the front to meet a prospective new home provider, she would panic, and bolt for the back. Most people don't want a cat like that, and it is important to me that we find just the right forever home for every cat that we place.

Iris had overstayed her welcome. We loved her. She was the sweetest thing. But although the entire community now feels they can bring stray cats to us, we really are not a humane society! I needed to find a home for her, one that she would like. My techs were saturated with pets and although some would have certainly made room for Iris, I did not want her to live stressed in the presence of other animals.

Once again, Animal Communicator to the rescue? Maybe Rebecca could help us convince Iris to be friendly to her visitors. During their session, Iris wanted to tell Rebecca what she remembered about her former home. She could picture a big brick building and a big green dumpster. She had two little girls that she loved, and she wanted them back again. How sad.

Now, I was on a mission to find two little girls for Iris. I put the word out to our clientele. No one could even visit or consider Iris for their pet, unless they had two little girls in their family and no other pets. A lot of time passed.
One day, I came into the clinic and my staff was smiling, they whispered, "Dr. Jodie, look, Iris is upfront rubbing and purring in the laps of two little girls who just came in to meet her! She has picked them! She is not running away. She is really happy!"

It was love at first site for the entire merry band. After months of waiting, Iris found the forever home that she was waiting for. The human-animal bond is magical.

Your Pet Cares Mork and Me

Pets do have wants and emotional needs regarding the characteristics of their guardian(s) and even their guardian's well-being. Remember in the Dedication I mentioned that when my soul dog, Mork, spoke to Rebecca his first utterings were of concern for me. He could sense that I was rushed and sad. He told Rebecca that I would run into the house, throw their food together and then sit on the couch and watch TV. He could have added that I was impatient and no fun and that all I wanted to do was lose myself in a mind-numbing soap opera. When Rebecca made me aware of that level of concern that Mork had for me and how my attitude was noticeable to him. I knew I had to change, for my sake and for his. We began going to a local indoor pool for dogs.

This experience changed our relationship forever. It brought both of us such joy. I would throw a ball or squeaky toy into that water over and over. Mork would wiggle his little tail stub trying to figure out the best way to enter the water. Then swim gallantly to rescue the item and return it only to repeat again and again until our time was up. Mork had arthritis and it made me feel so good to know how much this exercise was benefitting him.

I think he knew how much this experience was benefitting me by getting me out of the house to go somewhere other than work! Standing by that pool, especially in the wintertime, was like a mini vacation.

In Chapter 8 we will talk a bit more about all the things you can do to address self-care for the sake of yourself and your pet!

CHAPTER 5

Yummy Food! *Species Appropriate Nutrition*

Please open your mind before you open your pet's mouth! Since when is dry kibble dog or cat food? If you could ask your mini carnivores what diets they were meant to consume, wouldn't they answer, "…a rabbit please, I'd like some chicken; please put a mouse on my plate!"

What is species appropriate nutrition and why is it vitally important? What should a carnivore eat and who gets to decide? Every book, every article, every blog post on nutrition seems to say something different, often contradictory to the one you read before. Which expert, which resource should you believe? I didn't know either when I first began my quest for the best foods to feed my pets and pet patients. Then I decided to put each suggestion through one simple test. What makes sense in nature? Can I justify a food ingredient, supplement, or treat by asking if a dog or cat would eat this in nature? As you do this, keep in mind the artificial restrictions we put on our pets regarding allowing them access to nature. Let us begin with some basics about so-called pet foods.

The Nutritional Ladder™

During my holistic veterinary career, I have taught natural nutrition as steps up the ladder. At the bottom of the ladder are generic brands of dry, processed kibble, next up are grocery store brands, above those are the so-called premium brands. Closer to the top are those which claim natural status. Above them are the canned diets which are quality meat and moisture-filled and contain minimal to no grain. At the top are home-prepared cooked or raw commercial balanced diets. To determine where your pet's diet fits on the Nutritional Ladder™, it is helpful to learn how to read an ingredient label. There is an art, a science, and an awareness of the tricks necessary to accurately decipher this!

How to Read an Ingredient Label

Ingredients are more important than the minimums and maximums of protein, fat, fiber, and moisture identified on the analysis panel. This panel is very misleading. Do you realize that carbohydrates are not even listed in the guaranteed analysis? Do you know that leather meal (i.e., animal hide) is high protein? [2] Do you know that the more moisture in the food the lower the protein content will appear? Can you calculate how digestible the food is based on the label information? Remember, it is not that you are what you eat, but rather what you absorb! What is AAFCO and why do we look for their approval on a package of pet food?

AAFCO

AAFCO is the Association of American Feed Control Officials, an industry organization. Consumers have been trained to believe that a pet food is complete and balanced for all life stages if it says on the bag: "This food meets or exceeds AAFCO nutrient profiles and is suitable for all life stages."

But, here is what AAFCO says, *"It is impossible that any list of concentrations can invariably ensure that all nutrient requirements are fulfilled in all diet formulas without additional considerations. As stated for the previous editions of the AAFCO Dog and Cat Food Nutrient Profiles, formulating a product according to the Profiles is only one part of a nutritionally sound, scientific development that must consider all other aspects of the product. The fact that a dog or cat food is formulated to meet a specific AAFCO Profile should not deter or discourage the manufacturer from conducting appropriate feeding trials to further confirm and ensure the diet is nutritionally adequate for its intended use."* [3]

Thankfully, better standards are being developed. But, still with all this in mind, learning some AAFCO definitions and labeling tricks can help you compare foods and choose what diet may be the best for your situation. Incidentally, there is no AAFCO definition for Premium or Natural! This terminology was made up by the manufacturers themselves.

Back of the Bag
Order and Definitions

Always look at the back of the bag or the side of the box for "Ingredients:" They are listed in order of weight.

Meat

Ideally, we want to see a meat first. This refers to clean flesh. Look for a specific meat such as pork or beef. If it is listed as such, it has been weighed with the water still in it. This makes it heavier and brings it to the top of the list. However, the water is removed in processing, meaning less weight of actual meat-derived protein in the food, so another term a "specific meat" meal is rendered tissues (no hair, hoof, hide nor extraneous materials) and by definition, up to 9% of the crude protein in the product may be pepsin indigestible. This product would be more protein dense than the counterpart weighed with water included however, it was rendered, not slaughtered.

By-products by definition are non-rendered, from slaughtered animals. They include organs, fat, and entrails, **not** hair, horns, teeth, or hooves. By-products can be healthy, but we don't know the quality based on a label listing. Carnivores **do** need to ingest organs for good health.

If a meat product is followed by more than one grain, than there may be more grain than meat by weight, even though the meat is listed first.

Grains

A common marketing trick is to list a grain, for example corn, as a breakdown of corn gluten, corn starch, corn middlings etc. This then puts the corn versions below the meat source unless you add them all together!

Corn is used to fatten livestock. Why? Corn is starchy. Starch is a carbohydrate or sugar. The storage form of excess carbohydrate in the body is triglycerides. Triglycerides are fat. Fat is the storage form of excess carbs. Carbs make you fat, not fat! Corn is not a natural food for a carnivore diet. Think about it!

In a presentation I attended, a Purina rep listed wheat as a common allergen. Why is it a major ingredient in their "Milk Bones®"?

INGREDIENTS:
Wheat flour, beef meal and beef bone meal, milk, wheat bran, beef fat preserved with tocopherols, salt, dicalcium phosphate wheat germ, natural flavor, calcium carbonate, brewers dried yeast, malted barley flour, vitamins (choline chloride, di-alpha tocopheryl acetate [vitamin E], vitamin A acetate, calcium pantothenate, riboflavin, vitamin B12 supplement, d-activated animal sterol [source of vitamin D3]), sodium metabisulfite (dough conditioner), minerals (zinc sulfate, copper sulfate, ethylenediamine dihydriodide [source of iodine]).

Soy has long been regarded by veterinarians as a common allergen. Today, most soy is of genetically modified origin, which is now being linked to cancer.[4,5]

Based on my observations, rice is gluten free and is a better choice for many pets than other grains. However, the processing and the high starch are still not ideal. There have also been reports about arsenic in rice.[6] Some GI signs improve or even resolve only to recur with repetitive use. Millet is a better digested grain, but also a source of starch.[7]

Grain-free Marketing Trick

Do not be fooled by "grain-free" diets. This does not mean starch free. The grain is commonly replaced by starchy potato or tapioca. Processed carbohydrates create inflammation.[8] Starch is "dampening" according to oriental philosophy. To make kibble, there must be a starch source.

"Grain-free" diets are often higher protein, which could be a positive or negative, so be aware. Many allergic dermatitis or inflammatory bowel pets do improve on these diets, but many do not. Improvement is often short-lived, simply due to a change in nutrients.

Fat and Preservatives

Next on a label, a fat is listed, ideally, specifically chicken fat, and how it is preserved (i.e. with mixed tocopherols, a source of vitamin E) vs avoid, animal fat (from any mammal) preserved with BHA, BHT, or ethoxyquin which have been shown to be carcinogenic in rats.[9] Ethoxyquin is banned in Europe, Australia and New Zealand.[10]

Added Sugars

Avoid added sugars such as corn syrup, molasses, beet sugar, and maple syrup. These are not useful nutrients. They entice your pet to eat the food, and to become addicted to it. Why? So you buy it! Just because your pet likes it, does not mean it is good for him!

Extra Salt

Salt should not be too high up on the list, which is often the case in canned foods. This is also addicting. It is exceedingly difficult to get a cat off an addictive canned diet. This often takes a 21-day addiction program! Taste buds will adjust, however. Plan to be patient!

Synthetic Vitamins and Minerals

If vitamins and minerals are added, look for vitamins and minerals which are chelated. This improves absorption. It will read 'something' chelate or 'something' proteinate. However, beware this chelation is not 'natural' and often occurs by combining a mineral with soy proteinate and the soy is most assuredly GMO soy.[11] Reminder, GMO seeds result in crops laden with pesticides, a means for pesticides to be incorporated in to our gut microflora.[12]

Good Stuff at the End of the Label

Small amounts of the best, healthiest, and most expensive ingredients are usually last! These look like real foods.

You may see blueberries, cranberries, broccoli, dried kelp, hemp seed and more. Some foods, like chicory root extract are prebiotics which promote gut flora health. Prebiotics feed probiotics-the good bacteria. You might also see prebiotics on the label as inulin; this can come from chicory root.[13]

Added probiotics may not be as viable as adding them yourself to the food when serving, but I applaud company attempts to include these, although paying more for them may be a waste of money.[14] These will have long names like *Lactobacillus acidophilus and Bifidobacteria.*

Dye

Lastly, if a food contains dye (i.e., red dye 40), run![15]

I decided to include here the exact public information from the AAFCO site regarding label terminology. There has been so much confusion regarding this. In the end, it doesn't matter because it all pertains to processed food, which is all crap. But I realize society demands that kibble and canned be available for dogs and cats, so there will always be some who feed this. Information is power. So, if you the consumer know what you are buying then you can make an educated choice and choose better.

AAFCO Definitions with their explanations:
(http://www.aafco.org/Consumers/What-is-in-Pet-Food)[16]

"**Meat** is the clean flesh derived from slaughtered mammals and is limited to that part of the striate muscle which is skeletal or that part which is found in the tongue, in the diaphragm, in the heart or in the esophagus; with or without the accompanying and overlying fat and portions of the skin, sinew, nerve, and blood vessels which normally accompany the flesh. It shall be suitable for animal food. If it bears a name descriptive of its kind, it must correspond thereto."

In other words, "meat" is primarily the muscle tissue of the animal, but may include the fat, gristle and other tissues normally accompanying the muscle, like what you might see in a portion of raw meat sold for human consumption. This may include the less appealing cuts of meat, including the heart muscle and the muscle that separates the heart and lungs from the rest of the internal organs, but it is still muscle tissue. However, it does not include bone. Meat for pet food often is "mechanically separated," a process where the muscle is stripped from the bone by machines, resulting in a finely ground product with a paste-like consistency (similar to what might be used in hot dogs).

In addition to using the term "meat," the pet food manufacturer may also identify the species from which the meat is derived, such as "beef" or "pork." However, to use the generic term "meat" on the label, it can only be from cattle, pigs, sheep or goats. If it comes from any other mammal, the species must be identified (for example, "buffalo" or "venison"), so you can rest easy that if any other species was used, it would have to be declared. Also, if the muscle is from non-mammalian species, such as poultry or fish, it cannot be declared as "meat" but must use the appropriate identifying terms.

"**Meat by-products** is the non-rendered, clean parts, other than meat, derived from slaughtered mammals. It includes, but is not limited to, lungs, spleen, kidneys, brain, livers, blood, bone, partially de-fatted low temperature fatty tissue, and stomachs and intestines freed of their contents. It does not include hair, horns, teeth and hoofs. It shall be suitable for use in animal feed. If it bears a name descriptive of its kind, it must correspond thereto."

To put it another way, it is most of the parts of the animal other than the muscle tissue, including the internal organs and bones. It includes some of the parts people eat (such as livers, kidneys and tripe), but also parts that are not typically consumed by humans in the US. Some by-products, like udders and lungs are not deemed "edible" by USDA for human consumption, but they can be perfectly safe and nutritious for animals not inclined to be swayed by the unappealing nature of these parts of animals. As with "meat," unless the by-products are derived from cattle, pigs, sheep or goats, the species must be identified.

"**Poultry** is the clean combination of flesh and skin with or without accompanying bone, derived from the parts or whole carcasses of poultry or a combination thereof, exclusive of feathers, heads, feet and entrails. It shall be suitable for use in animal food. If it bears a name

48

descriptive of its kind, it must correspond thereto. If the bone has been removed, the process may be so designated by use of the appropriate feed term."

In other words, it is the parts of the bird as you would find if you purchased a whole chicken or turkey at the grocery store. Frankly, it often consists of the less profitable parts of the bird, such as backs and necks. Unlike "meat," it may include the bone, which when ground can serve as a good source of calcium. If the bone has been removed (typically by mechanical separation), however, it can be declared as "deboned poultry." If a particular species of bird is used, it may be declared by the more common name, such as "chicken" or "turkey."

"Poultry By-Products must consist of non-rendered clean parts of carcasses of slaughtered poultry such as heads, feet, viscera, free from fecal content and foreign matter except in such trace amounts as might occur unavoidably in good factory practice. If the product bears a name descriptive of its kind, it must correspond thereto."

Similar to "meat by-products," it is most of the parts of the bird that would not be part of a raw, dressed whole carcass. That may include the giblets (heart, gizzard, and liver) but also other internal organs, heads and feet.

The following materials are all rendered products that have been subject to cooking to destroy any harmful bacteria before they are shipped to a pet food manufacturing plant. Rendering is a process where the materials are subject to heat and pressure, removing most of the water and fat and leaving primarily protein and minerals. You will notice that the term "meal" is used in all cases; because, in addition to cooking, the products are ground to form uniform sized particles.

"Meat Meal is the rendered product from mammal tissues, exclusive of any added blood, hair, hoof, horn, hide trimmings, manure, stomach and rumen contents except in such amounts as may occur unavoidably in good processing practices. It shall not contain extraneous materials not provided for by this definition. .... {the definition goes on to include the required mineral specifications and required nutrient guarantees} ..... If the product bears a name descriptive of its kind, composition, or origin it must correspond thereto."

The rendering process is designed to destroy disease-causing bacteria, leaving an ingredient high in protein that while unappetizing to people appeals to the carnivore's palate. Unlike "meat" and "meat by-products," this ingredient may be from mammals other than cattle, pigs, sheep or goats without further description. However, a manufacturer may designate a species if appropriate (such as "beef meal" if only from cattle).

"**Meat and Bone Meal** is the rendered product from mammal tissues, including bone, exclusive of any added blood, hair, hoof, horn, hide trimmings, manure, stomach and rumen contents except in such amounts as may occur unavoidably in good processing practices. It shall not contain extraneous materials not provided for by this definition. …. {the definition goes on to include the required mineral specifications and required nutrient guarantees}….. If the product bears a name descriptive of its kind, composition or origin it must correspond thereto."

Similar to "meat meal," but can include added bone in addition to what is normally found in whole carcasses.

"**Animal By-Product Meal** is the rendered product from mammal tissues, exclusive of any added hair, hoof, horn, hide trimmings, manure, stomach and rumen contents except in such amounts as may occur unavoidably in good processing practices. It shall not contain extraneous materials not provided for by this definition. This ingredient definition is intended to cover those individual rendered animal tissues that cannot meet the criteria as set forth elsewhere in this section. This ingredient is not intended to be used to label a mixture of animal tissue products."

May consist of whole carcasses, but often includes by-products in excess of what would normally be found in "meat meal" and "meat and bone meal."

"**Poultry By-Product Meal** consists of the ground, rendered clean parts of the carcasses of slaughtered poultry such as necks, feet, undeveloped eggs and intestines, exclusive of feathers except in such amounts as might occur unavoidably in good processing practices…..{the definition goes on to include the required mineral specifications and required nutrient guarantees}….. If the product bears a name descriptive of its kind, it must correspond thereto."

Essentially the same as "poultry by-products," but in rendered form so most of the water and fat has been removed to make a concentrated protein/mineral ingredient.

"**Poultry Meal** is the dry rendered product from a combination of clean flesh and skin with or without accompanying bone, derived from the parts or whole carcasses of poultry or a combination thereof, exclusive of feathers, heads, feet and entrails. It shall be suitable for use in animal food. If it bears a name descriptive of its kind, it must correspond thereto."

Basically the same as "poultry," but in rendered form, so most of the water and fat has been removed to make a concentrated protein/mineral ingredient.

Some other ingredients
Animal and vegetable fats or oils are commonly used to supply additional energy and flavor to a pet food.
Plant ingredients like corn, barley, peas, and potatoes also supply energy and help hold kibbles together.
There are a number of sources of dietary fiber used in pet food, including dried beet pulp, dried chicory root, fructooligosaccharide, powdered cellulose, and inulin.

What are some of the ingredients used to supply vitamins and minerals in a pet food?
There are many inorganic compounds used to supply minerals and most of them can be identified by what they supply with names beginning with elements such as calcium, cobalt, copper, ferric or ferrous (meaning Iron), magnesium, manganese, potassium, sodium, or zinc. Others may have the mineral as part of the second half of the name, such as "___iodate" (for iodine) or "___selenite (for selenium). Some may include two useful minerals, such as "dicalcium phosphate" (supplying both calcium and phosphorus).

There are several classes of synthetic mineral ingredients that are called metal amino acid complexes, metal amino acid chelates and polysaccharide complexes. You may see specific designations, for example, "Iron Amino Acid Complex", "Magnesium amino acid chelate" or "Zinc polysaccharide complex". The theory behind these synthesized ingredients is improved bioavailability compared to strictly inorganic mineral compounds.

Some examples of ingredients used to provide vitamin activity include such materials as Cholecalciferol (supplies vitamin D from animal sources), Ergocalciferol (supplies vitamin D from plant sources), Vitamin B12 supplement, Riboflavin supplement (a source of vitamin B2), Vitamin A supplement, Vitamin D3 supplement, alpha-Tocopherol acetate (supplies vitamin E), Thiamine mononitrate (source of vitamin B1) and pyridoxine hydrochloride (source of vitamin B6). That is far from all of the ingredients used to supply vitamin activity, but enough to give you an idea.

What about some of the other ingredients used in pet foods with "chemical sounding" names?
Some additives which supply amino acids: DL-Methionine, L-Lysine, L-Threonine, DL-Tryptophan, Taurine (particularly important to cats), DL-Arginine, L-Tyrosine.

Some ingredients which function as chemical preservatives: Ascorbic acid, Benzoic acid, Butylated hydroxyl anisol (BHA), Butylated hydroxyltoluene (BHT), Calcium ascorbate, Citric acid, Ethoxyquin, Potassium sorbate, Sodium bisulfate, Mixed Tocopherols. Some of these preservatives have limits to the amount that can be used or what types of products the preservative can be added to. The fact that a preservative has been added must be shown, such as preserved with BHT or mixed tocopherols (preservative).

Other ingredients you may find on an ingredient list that are often used as conditioning agents, thickeners, emulsifiers, sequestrants, flavors and seasonings might include:
Carrageenan, propylene glycol (in dog food only, propylene glycol is unsafe for cats and is prohibited from use in cat food), sodium hexametaphosphate (dental – tartar reduction in dogs and cats), agar-agar, and guar gum.
There are a large number of spices and extracts that are used for flavorings. Some examples include ginger, chamomile, fennel, rosemary, and several extracts of commonly known plants.

I did not add, delete, nor change one word of this. This information has been miscommunicated and misinterpreted time and again. I felt that it was important for you, my client to read this, if desired, in its entirety. I am not a fan of processed foods at all. However, I think it is important for individuals to make decisions based on accurate information.

Many informed consumers have become frustrated with poor quality kibble diets and all the recent recalls. There has been a trend toward fresher food options and even raw, prey-concept feeding. Many commercial, quality, balanced, and convenient-to-feed raw products exist!

Nature's Intent

I base my current opinions on my disappointing first decade of veterinary practice which included recommending veterinary prescription and "premium" diets. Successful outcomes were not satisfactory. We were taught to tell clients that prescription diets do not always work, and indeed, they did not! During my second and now third decades of practice, I have been recommending and feeding with measurable success, the more natural options at the top of the Nutritional Ladder™. To my now open mind, this theory of feeding carnivorous pets, a more natural meat-based, prey-concept diet is common sense!

As I discuss this topic, which can be overwhelming to grasp at first, just remember when you become confused by all the dietary recommendations that may barrage you from other sources, ask yourself, "What did nature intend for this species to eat?"

Think about it. Our companion dogs and cats are carnivores. Cats are strict carnivores. Dogs are slightly more omnivorous. We are primates. Our bodies are not biologically designed to eat the same things.

We chew our food and mix it with saliva. This is an important break-down process which aids proper digestion of vegetation. A rabbit has an enzyme called cellulase which can break down cell walls of plants to release nutrients to be utilized by the rabbit.[17] We, and our carnivorous pets, do not have this enzyme, so we chew our veggies.

What does a dog need to do? Eat the rabbit of course! A cat won't eat peas and carrots, and a carrot fed to a dog comes out the other end undigested! Your kitty or dog can assimilate vitamins when consumed in a pre-digested form as they are in the gut of the prey. The prey has gently blended and warmed the vegetation which releases the healthy *whole food source* vitamins and minerals for your pet. Look for more on this later.

So, the premise of those who aspire to feed quality, balanced diets to their pet companions is to mimic nature as closely as they are able to do.

An accomplished holistic veterinarian, Dr. Robert Silver, feeds whole dead quail to his cats. This is surely balanced prey-concept feeding and certainly a leap to the top of my Nutritional Ladder™! But for most of us, there are, thankfully, other healthy steps on the ladder which are more convenient and "palatable" to us.

I will have more to say on quail and cats later, when we talk about raw bones!

Balanced Diets?

I am an options person. I believe there is no perfect commercial diet. I assert that you can improve upon any pet's diet with a step up the ladder, with proper supplementation and by feeding variety.

If we eat the same meal day after day, we will perhaps unknowingly repeat the same excess or deficiency over and over! In time, this effect can be devastating to one's health.

For many years, we have been told that AAFCO approved pet foods are 100% complete – balanced for all life stages of our pets. We were told to choose a brand and follow the feeding guideline for cups per day based on our pets' weight. This would provide the proper nutrition for our companion to "thrive" for a lifetime. What we have learned is this feeding method will provide ingredients for our companion to "survive", but often with chronic disease. Even AAFCO emphasizes to manufacturers when using their nutrient profiles as guidelines for making diets, *"processing may destroy up to 90% of the thiamine in the diet, allowances in formulation should be made to ensure the minimum nutrient concentration for thiamine is met after processing"*.[18]

Research has shown these balanced diets initially contained inadequate taurine. Many cats developed a heart disorder which is preventable with adequate taurine.[19] Now, by law, processed pet food manufacturers must add taurine to their diets. Where in nature is taurine found? Raw meat of course, especially heart muscle. Taurine is lost in the high heat processing of kibble and canned diets.

Getting overwhelmed? Ask yourself, what would a cat eat in nature? A cat would eat a mouse of course! Mice are very high in taurine. Interesting!

So ideally a carnivore should eat meat that is *uncooked* because processing destroys nutrients they need to thrive.

Which nutrients have researchers not yet discovered to be lacking in "balanced" kibble? What diseases could be prevented or treated if we knew what to add or decrease?

The basic goal of good nutrition is to prevent or treat disease. Remove from the diet ingredients we know or suspect to be harmful and add to the diet things that we know, or suspect could be helpful. To be your pets' advocate in this quest, some basic knowledge of how to read pet food packaging and what are the components of the prey-concept is required.

The Prey Concept

A carcass contains four major components: **flesh, organs, bone, and vegetation** from the stomach. These items are essential to the proper balancing of a home-prepared or commercial raw diet.

When raw diet proponents say they feed a meat diet, accurately they intend to promote the prey concept. Dr. Ian Billinghurst, an Australian holistic veterinarian, coined the term BARF diet, which refers to Biologically Appropriate Raw Food.

Many veterinarians are fearful of this concept and harass their clients for feeding this diet because they are unaware of the appropriateness of this diet when prepared properly. Many veterinarians have witnessed the feeding of meat scraps and *cooked* bones which have led to illness or death in many pets. Cooked or excessive fat can cause diarrhea or pancreatitis. Cooked bones are indigestible and can lodge in or perforate intestines. This is not intelligent prey-concept feeding.
I counsel my clients who choose to feed a home-prepared raw diet to follow a recipe and menu plan by an author who has demonstrated over generations of animals that their plan is balanced and successful. It is imperative to follow one proven plan. Don't leave out important components. Some "internet diets" may not be "proven."

Home preparation will require feeding lots of whole raw bones or grinding bone or properly adding a calcium supplement to balance the high phosphorous in the meat. Raw feeding does <u>not</u> mean adding pieces of meat to kibble. This is not a balanced diet. There is only enough calcium in the kibble diet to balance or offset the phosphorous which is in the meat in the kibble, NOT the additional meat that you mix with it. This is a common error.

If you purchase a commercial raw diet which has been analyzed by a veterinary animal nutritionist, then the balancing has been done for you. Remember, there is no perfect diet, so variety, even among raw diet brands, is key! Commercial raw diets are not all the same. Each provide the **four prey components (flesh, bone, organs, vegetation)** in different ways, different proportions, different product consistencies, different packaging. Each has a niche. I utilize ten different brands in my practice. Each brand comes in several different meat varieties as well. Some are produced in separate dog or cat versions. It is helpful to purchase these products where you can receive guidance as to which brand, which meat variety, which packaging may be best for your situation.

You should have several in-depth conversations with those who are experienced in raw feeding about brand selection, gradual transition, amounts to feed, utensils to use, food temperature and preparation. When you become comfortable with the concept and experience, commercial raw diet feeding is simple! This is the easiest way to start. A balanced home-prepared menu is more complicated but may be a necessary goal for financial reasons if your household includes many small carnivores or a couple of large ones!

What's Excessive?

Remember, mimic nature. Take out of the diet what is bad. Put in what is good.

Commercial, heat-processed kibble diets are full of processed grains. Do dogs and cats eat processed corn, wheat, soy or rice when they live outside on their own? No. They eat rabbits, birds, mice, maybe some fish. So, take out the processed grains. In nature, herbivores eat undigested vegetation. Livestock are fed processed grains to warm them in the winter and fatten them for slaughter. Our carnivores cannot metabolize excessive carbohydrates, and this causes excessive weight gain!

Your fat dog does not need a low fat, high fiber diet. He needs a high protein, low carbohydrate diet. The Atkins of the past, the Paleo of today, perhaps best of all, a ketogenic diet[20] are the types to be analyzing for our carnivores. For many of the same reasons as in humans, these moderate-protein, high quality fat, low- carbohydrate diets are preventative and management for many afflictions, including obesity, seizures, allergies and cancer. Obese dogs are more prone to arthritis. Obese cats often become diabetic. Get rid of the sugar!

Dental Health

We have all been misled to believe that dry food is good for our pets' teeth. In reality, eating kibble is like crunching on sugar cubes.

Most dogs on dry diets develop gingivitis, periodontal disease and still need professional dental scaling and extractions several times during their lives.

Cats are very prone to dental cavities. They lose their teeth at young ages due to cavities requiring extractions. To make kibble, it is necessary to put excessive starchy carbohydrates into the food. These break down into sugar!

Researchers in South America noticed that children working in sugar cane fields all day chewed on fresh sugar cane and had beautiful, white teeth! Yet American children who consume the processed sugar develop dental disease. It was concluded that chemicals involved in processing the sugar are detrimental to oral health! [21]

Likewise, those who prepare home-cooked diets are often successful utilizing some healthy cooked grains in their pets' diets, versus problems seen with comparable highly processed grains utilized in commercial kibble.

Many conventional as well as holistic veterinarians have become aware that the removal of processed grains is necessary to prevent a variety of inflammatory disorders in our pets such as periodontal disease, chronic otitis in dogs, facial pruritus in cats, and inflammatory bowel disease. I have seen a correlation between excessive sugar intake and pancreatitis. A sugary biscuit treat can be blamed just as easily as the cheese or grease which is commonly demonized as the inciting stimulus for this serious disorder. Raw bones provide prevention and treatment.

Cancer is Fueled by Carbs

Hill's developed their neoplasia diet based on a study by Dr. Greg Ogilvie, which compared two groups of dogs with lymphoma (a far too common cancer). Both groups were treated with similar cancer therapy protocols.

One group was fed dry kibble. The other group was fed a moist, meat-based diet. The group fed the meat diet with more fat and protein and less sugar than the dry kibble eaters had better quality of life and more longevity as well! This study performed by a conventional diet manufacturer demonstrated, what is now a commonly held belief, cancer feeds on carbs.[22]

Guaranteed Analysis

Just how much sugar is in your pet's dry, processed kibble diet? Wouldn't it be nice if they told you on the label? They don't have to, so they don't! You will need to do a simple calculation to figure this out. Read the back of the bag or the side panel and look for the Guaranteed Analysis. **Add up four things: percent moisture, percent fat, percent protein, and lastly percent fiber**. There may be a few other things, but their overall percent will be negligible. You can add them in too if you would like. After you add these major four, **subtract the total from 100. The resultant number is the percent carbohydrate** (starch/sugar) in that bag. It will be about 50 %. The best I have seen was 37%, some as high as 60%. One-third to over half of the bag is sugar.

Do you want half of your pet's diet to be sugar?

Grain-Free

Have you heard that grain-free is better? It is meatier, right? This is the worst marketing trick perpetuated by the pet food industry of our decade! Grains are simply replaced by alternative starches such as potato or millet. Grain-free does not mean starch free, and starch is the culprit. In fact, sometimes the potato starch is even worse.

Potato

Potato is in the Nightshade family of plants, a common allergenic group. Also, most of America's potato crops are of genetically modified origin (GMO). There is some evidence that some potato may provide to the gut what is being called 'resistant starch'. This may slow sugar absorption, pass through the gut itself, unabsorbed, and help with weight loss.

One source cited blue potatoes as being high in this beneficial form of starch. There are 4 different types of resistant starch. The preparation method has a major effect on the ultimate amount of resistant starch in food. [23] In my practice, I believe the highly processed potato starch found in kibble diets is not beneficial and is actually correlated with weight gain and obesity in dogs and cats.

Quiz for You

Here is another example. Can you do the math? Calculate the % carbohydrate and try to identify toxins in the ingredient list and explain why. How many toxins can you find in this dry kibble diet? This is a top-selling grocery store product. Can you guess the brand?

INGREDIENTS: *Ground yellow corn, chicken by-product meal, corn gluten meal, whole wheat flour, animal fat preserved with mixed-tocopherols, rice flour, beef, soy flour, meat and bone meal, propylene glycol, sugar, tricalcium phosphate, salt, phosphoric acid, potassium chloride, animal digest, sorbic acid (a preservative), mono and dicalcium phosphate, dried spinach, dried peas, dried carrots, L-Lysine monohydrochloride, calcium propionate (a preservative), choline chloride, zinc sulfate, Vitamin E supplement, ferrous sulfate, manganese sulfate, Red 40, niacin, Vitamin A supplement, Yellow 6, Yellow 5, copper sulfate, Vitamin B-12 supplement, calcium pantothenate, Blue 2, thiamine mononitrate, garlic oil, pyridoxine hydrochloride, riboflavin supplement, Vitamin D-3 supplement, calcium iodate, menadione sodium bisulfite complex (source of Vitamin K activity), folic acid, biotin, sodium selenite.*

GUARANTEED ANALYSIS:

23.0%	Crude **Protein** *(min)*	1.0% *Calcium (Ca) (min)*
10.0%	Crude **Fat** *(min)*	0.2 mg/kg *Selenium (Se) (min)*
4.0%	Crude **Fiber** *(max)*	10,000 IU/kg *Vitamin A (min)*
14.0%	**Moisture** *(max)*	100 IU/kg *Vitamin E (min)*
1.5%	Linoleic Acid *(min)*	

Here's the math:
23 + 10 + 4 + 14 = 51%
100% - 51% = 49% **Carbohydrate**

Almost half of the bag is sugar! We wonder why so many dogs are obese! Make it all better and balanced by adding vitamins, right? No!

Synthetic Vitamins and Minerals

Can you identify the synthetic vitamins and minerals in the bag? Synthetics are laboratory derived. Real nutrients should sound like foods, not chemicals!

A whole food source is a complex puzzle of vitamins, minerals and co-factors which are recognized and utilized safely and efficiently by the body!

Synthetic, lab derived	Whole Food Source
Vitamin C, ascorbic acid, calcium ascorbate	Rose hips, kale, berries
Vitamin E, d-alpha tocopherol, tocopheryl	Wheat germ oil
Selenium, sodium selenite	Brazil nuts

If you look at an ingredient label and many of the ingredients sound like chemicals, they likely are. Food ingredients should be recognizable as foods!

Grab a bag of kibble. If it calls itself "natural," it quite likely also states "with added vitamins and minerals." AAFCO requires this statement because the vitamins and minerals are synthetic, not natural. The group is usually listed in the middle to bottom of the ingredient label, as all ingredients are listed in order of weight. Most of the names will sound like chemicals.

Following is a typical sample "natural" brand *with added vitamins and minerals:*

Chicken, Chicken Meal, Brown Rice, Oats, Barley, Rice, Menhaden Fish Meal, Chicken Fat (preserved with mixed tocopherols) Natural Chicken Flavors, Flaxseed, Dried Egg Product, Potatoes, Carrots, Herring, Natural Flavors, Whole Eggs, Apples, Carrots, Sweet Potatoes, Herring Oil, Dried Kelp, Potassium Chloride, Dicalcium Phosphate, Salt, Garlic, Vitamin E Supplement, (various fermentation products), Calcium Carbonate, Choline Chloride, Zinc Sulfate, Vitamin A Supplement, Vitamin D3 Supplement, Ferrous Sulfate, Copper Sulfate, Manganese Sulfate, Niacin, Calcium Pantothenate, Vitamin B12 Supplement, Folic Acid, Riboflavin, Sodium Selenite, Pyridoxine Hydrochloride, Calcium Iodate, Thiamine Mononitrate, Biotin, Cobalt Sulfate, Rosemary Extract.

Unnatural vs Natural, Does it Matter?

Let's analyze just one mineral out of the above list of synthetic additives: sodium selenite.

Sodium selenite contains **selenium**. When we eat natural, unprocessed, whole foods such as nuts, meat, mushrooms, fish, or eggs, we eat selenium that is complexed and consumed along with other nutrients which help the selenium function properly in the body.

"Humans and animals derive selenium primarily from foods. In plants and animals, selenium is primarily localized in the protein fraction".[24] Brazil nuts are the richest dietary source of selenium. High levels of selenium are also found in kidney, tuna, crab, and lobster. But these foods contain selenium, not sodium selenite.

"Both mutagenic activity (cancer causing) and antimutagenic (cancer preventing) activity have been attributed to selenium; the concentration and the chemical form in which selenium is administered appear to be critical in determining its effects. At the trace levels normally found in biological systems (plants and animals), selenium apparently acts as an antimutagenic, oxygen-radical scavenger, but at higher concentrations selenium is capable of inducing mutations (cancer)."[25]

Where does sodium selenite come from anyway? Sodium selenite is prepared by evaporating an aqueous solution of sodium hydroxide (lye or drain cleaner) and selenous acid.[26] Selenous acid is produced by combining water and selenium dioxide which is produced during the industrial purification of copper.

Does this sound like something you want your pet to eat?

According to the National Institute for Occupational Safety and Health (NIOSH), *"prolonged exposure to sodium selenite may cause paleness, coated tongue, stomach disorders, nervousness, metallic taste and a garlic odor of the breath. Fluid in the abdominal cavity, damage to the liver and spleen and anemia have been reported in animals."*[27]

Do you know any pets with these disorders? How many times have you heard a pet parent comment that a change from kibble to fresh raw food improved the pet's breath? Interesting!

The selenium we want to eat is a trace element, which is a cofactor for reducing antioxidant enzymes, found in animals and most plants. This biologic source of selenium is crucial to the proper functioning of every cell in the body, especially the thyroid gland.

Selenium may inhibit Hashimoto's disease, the human version of autoimmune thyroiditis, which has reached epidemic levels in our dogs. Selenium can even reduce the effects of mercury toxicity.

Can cells recognize unnatural vitamin and mineral sources? In addition to the realization that unnatural sources of selenium can be toxic, their presence can inhibit the ability of natural sources to function properly in the body. Cells have receptor sites for the attachment of biologic factors which turn on and off cellular functions. These receptors can become "clogged" with look-alike vitamins or minerals.[28]

This phenomenon can explain why the initial consumption of a synthetic vitamin or mineral or even hormone replacement therapy works initially, when the receptor sites are empty, and desperate for the nutrient. But, when the receptors become clogged with the inadequately functioning faux nutrients, the cell receptors cannot function properly. You or your pet may feel great after beginning a new synthetic supplement, or even a new type of diet, only for the original symptoms to recur after some time passes.

It's important to remember that the problem doesn't start and end with selenium. Every synthetic vitamin and mineral carries similar risks and shortcomings.

The solution for the synthetic nutrient dilemma is in consumer demand. When most pet foods contained artificial preservatives (BHA, BHT, ethoxyquin), it was consumer pressure that drove the industry to manufacture their pet diets without them. It will likely be pet owner education and consumer demand that will again cause the industry to produce pet diets without these toxic vitamin and mineral additions. Many brands of raw food and at least one brand of kibble and canned already exist to fulfill this need.

One of the most devastating recalls in recent pet food history occurred when a reputable manufacturer accidentally dropped too much of a synthetic vitamin into the recipe. Dogs died. Generally, too much of a whole food source, like oranges or Brussels sprouts, will at worst cause some raging diarrhea but the body can recognize and purge the excess appropriately! Unfortunately, this normal body response may not occur with a synthetic counterpart, and death may be the result.

I can sleep well at night knowing that I am not feeding any foods to my pets which may contain an excess of a dangerous laboratory-derived vitamin! How about you?

What's Deficient?

There are four major nutrient categories that we know are deficient in heat-processed kibble or canned diets. There may be many other individual nutrients which are missing. The four categories are **probiotics, enzymes, fatty acids, and whole food source vitamins and minerals.**

If you purchase a healthy kitten or puppy and feed him or her, a **balanced raw diet**, with variety, there is rarely any need for supplementation. This is because **flesh, organs, ground bone and blended veggies** contain the four categories listed above. These components are especially important for proper digestion, a strong immune system, disease prevention and treatment.

If your pet has a particular disorder or genetic pre-disposition, you may need to supplement additional amounts of some of these categories even though you're utilizing a raw diet.

Probiotics/prebiotics/enzymes

Probiotics are good bacteria. They can "crowd out" bad bacteria and yeast overgrowth. Prebiotics feed probiotics. Prebiotics include things like chicory root (inulin) or FOS (fructooligosaccharides). These are work together to facilitate proper gut fermentation and digestion.[29] Enzymes break up proteins, fats,
 and starches so they can be absorbed. Probiotics and enzymes are destroyed by high temperatures, for example, in the processing of dry kibble and canned diets.

Leaky Gut

Human naturopaths use the term "leaky gut syndrome" when referring to the "holes" in the mucosal barrier between the gut lumen and blood vessels where nutrient absorption should properly occur within the small intestines. These "holes" are created when the bacterial flora and enzyme processes are inadequate and allow unhealthy invasions to occur.
These invasions may be due to viruses, bacteria, toxins, allergens, carcinogens, etc. This barrier is our body's main immune defense mechanism.

Probiotics and enzymes are two important components which facilitate the proper functioning of this intestinal defense.

When a protein is broken up properly into amino acids, it can be absorbed into the blood stream and processed properly by the liver. When a protein penetrates a "leaky gut" intact, it is perceived as foreign and can be attacked by the immune system. This may be manifested as inflammatory bowel disease or an allergic skin reaction. Thus, the link between what your pet eats and symptoms such as vomiting, diarrhea or itchy ears or skin! If you feed processed food, it is important to supplement probiotics and enzymes.

Many individual two or four-legged suffer from this "leaky gut" without knowing. It is often the deepest root of an allergy, environmental or food related. Symptoms may be itchy, red skin or an inflamed gastrointestinal system causing vomiting and/or diarrhea.

Arty's Sauer kraut

Fermented foods sound old-fashioned. But with the prevalence of leaky gut disorders in our society and the correlation of that affliction with immune, autoimmune and neurologic disease, many consumers have awakened to the benefits of fermented vegetables.

In my practice, we are having amazing success feeding quality, fresh sauer kraut to dogs and even the juice to cats! Our clinic cat, Arty had diarrhea for a year which was unresponsive to every treatment, natural and conventional. After two days eating one milliliter of jalapeno flavored Farmhouse brand fresh sauer kraut twice per day, Arty passed formed stool and this has continued since. If we run out, his problem recurs. Now we never forget to give Arty his sauer kraut. He enjoys caraway sauer kraut as well!

Omega 3's/Fatty Acids

Conventional medicine often suppresses inflammatory responses with steroidal or non-steroidal anti-inflammatory drugs. Good nutrition can provide natural anti-inflammatories, without side effects of drugs. A most widely accepted group of natural anti-inflammatories are the Omega-3 fatty acids. The best source of these for a carnivore is fish oil.

One could view some inflammation as a fatty acid deficiency. Fatty acids are destroyed in the heat processing of dry kibble or canned diets. If you feed kibble or canned diets, you should add fish oil. I prefer an independently tested, anchovy sardine oil blend. Smaller fish accumulate fewer toxins in them, than do the bigger fish. I am not a fan of salmon oil. Most are factory farmed or endangered.

Rancid fish oil is worse than none. So, purchase only what you will utilize quickly. If your fish oil is a liquid, store it in your refrigerator and use within three months. I recommend cod liver oil in the winter, and if your pet has cancer or a skin disorder. Krill oil is a good option for this purpose as well. The body oil vs. liver oil of fish is higher in Omega 3's, so use these more anti-inflammatory options for pets with arthritis.

Guess what? There is finally a test to see if your pet has an adequate EPA:DHA ratio. These are the important utilizable fatty acids. It is called an iFATS Score. There are a growing number of holistic vets offering this test.

Whole Food Vitamins/Superfoods

Most processed kibble and canned diets provide an AAFCO approved blend of vitamins and minerals. Most of these are synthetic and poorly absorbed. Some sources say only about 10% are absorbed. Some better dry kibble diets chelate the vitamins. You can recognize this on the label as something-proteinate. This process makes them about 40% absorbed. This is better but not good enough! And, as we discussed, this chelation, although it improves absorption, often adds a GMO soy proteinate, which is a roundabout way to end up with pesticides in the food.

Nutritionists tell us to eat more fresh fruits and vegetables. When we consume these, we chew them and mix them with our saliva. This break down process provides us with absorbable, whole food source vitamins and minerals. This is how we get vitamin A out of a carrot.

Remember the rabbit with the enzyme called cellulase which we primates do not possess? This enzyme breaks down the carrot for the rabbit so he can assimilate the vitamin A. Carnivores do not have cellulase either. So, what must your dog or cat do to get vitamin A? Eat the rabbit of course! In the gut of the prey are the pre-digested (blended) fruits and vegetables – a carnivore's ideal source of whole food, non-synthetic, well-absorbed vitamins, and minerals.

The body is designed to recognize whole food source vitamins and minerals. Providing extra synthetic vitamins and minerals could be detrimental. Therefore, do not add synthetic sources to commercial kibble or canned pet foods.

A discussion about synthetic vitamins and minerals falls under the "What's Excessive" *and* the "What's Deficient" categories. Why? In particular, the use of synthetics can easily cause an excess or a deficiency.

Some are Good, More are Better?

Recently, David Waters, PhD, the keynote speaker at the American Holistic Veterinary Medical Association convention and a Ted Talk presenter, explained the seriousness of understanding that medications, supplements and vitamins and minerals metabolize in our bodies based upon a U-shaped curve. I love this explanation! The bottom of the U is the appropriate amount; the top of the U could be detrimental if deficient or excessive. He emphasized that more is not always better! [30]

In our decaying world where soils devoid of nutrients are producing plants and animals with vitamin and mineral deficiencies, we must realize the solution is NOT to fill the gap with synthetics, but rather seek out whole food sources.

Whole food supplementation will always be safest. Give our bodies and our pet's bodies the nutritional tools that they can recognize in order to utilize the amounts that they need. There is this thing called "bioindividuality" which we will discuss more in Chapter 8. But, basically, different individuals will thrive on different diets and food items. Not one diet is perfect for every individual. A body needs food choice. This is true for humans and pets.

So, when we try to control what an individual consumes, we create digestive problems, which is a major root of all dis-ease. The simple statement, "consume a variety of fresh foods" is so taken for granted. All good dietary programs will have that statement at their core.

Because we control what our pets consume, even if it is *fresh,* some analysis may be important to ensure adequacy of nutrients. Just as processed diets can be analyzed for nutrient content, so too can fresh diets. But there are some limitations. Often the laboratory methodology cannot measure the presence of a natural nutrient in the same way that it can enumerate the synthetic version. So, it may be reported as inadequate.

The analyzing organization may also need to recognize that a body can thrive on smaller amounts of whole food source vitamins than it can on their synthetic counterparts.

Veggie Rock Stars

If the addition of a vitamin or mineral nutrient is necessary, it should ideally be added from a whole food source. Manufacturing processes exist which can *concentrate* the whole food vitamins available from **cruciferous vegetables, berries and herbs and other dark, leafy greens.**

Organ concentrates can also be used in commercial diets, as nutrient resources to prevent and repair a myriad of disorders by helping to balance the vitamins and minerals in a whole food manner. To improve upon a home prepared diet or a processed kibble or canned diet, YOU can add leftover <u>blended</u> fruits and vegetables. Your carnivore's body can recognize and absorb what it needs or excrete excess of *natural* nutrients.

With this practice, you will mimic what occurs in the stomach of the prey. Lightly cook, or steam veggies (especially cruciferous, as these are the gas producers) and blend them to release the nutrients for utilization by your little carnivore. Fresh, blended fruits and vegetables can provide probiotics and enzymes in addition to whole food vitamins and minerals.

My cancer patients who do the best have guardians who feed them a variety of warmed, blended, dark leafy greens. Make it easy on yourself. For convenience, make a batch; pour it into an ice cube tray and freeze. Pop out a cube each day to thaw. Heat it on the stove. (Of course, never microwave.) Then add this to the thawed, balanced meat diet to warm it slightly. (Remember prey is raw but not cold!) Repetitive cold food will damage "stomach yin", an oriental philosophy. This explains why some pets eat raw well, cold, initially, and then turn off of it.

Ideas for greens include: kale, bok choy, collard greens, green beans, cucumber, dandelion greens, parsley, arugula, broccoli, spinach and more. These are loaded with natural, health supportive, cancer-fighting antioxidants!

Don't even get me started on the fabulous benefits of blue green algae like **spirulina and chlorella**! My little liver shunt dog, Jetson gets his "chlorella cookies" every morning!

Of course, **avoid** grapes, raisins and onions as these are toxic to our pets!

To review: You can really improve upon any processed diet by adding some fresh foods. Add a probiotic such as yogurt. This is not always ideal, but some fresh food is generally better than none. Add fatty acids by dribbling on some fresh fish oil. Provide enzymes (Standard Process® Multizyme, Young Living® Essentialzyme or Detoxzyme, Prozyme™, others) and whole food source vitamins and minerals by adding a spoonful of warmed, blended vegetables. Fill in all the gaps with fresh, cold sauer kraut or sprouted seeds like Flora4™. Mimic your carnivore's desire to forage by tossing him a berry periodically!

Why don't all manufacturers use quality, whole food, and fresh ingredients? Manufacturers make what the consumer wants. They sometimes create a mind set to make the consumer want what they make. Many pet parents have a preconceived notion of what a *pet food* should cost and how convenient it must be to utilize it. This belief is what drives the success or failure of a pet food company.

Pet food costs are rising but loving pet parents have realized that healthy foods cost more and they are willing to pay for safe and effective supplements and food. As manufacturers realize there is a consumer need and willingness to purchase, they will respond by producing better and better pet diets. So, YOU have control!

Pet owners must continue to seek out nutritional education and not be swayed to purchase foods based just on low cost or influential marketing. Dog and cat lovers need to become aware of and support companies who produce ethically.

Purchase species appropriate, fresh foods and treats. Learn to read ingredient labels. Share this information with your family, friends, and fellow pet enthusiasts. Encourage your veterinarian and other pet providers to be open minded. Do not just accept the status quo. Disseminate information and ask good questions!

CHAPTER 6

Good Vet! *Integrative Veterinary Care*

You might explain to Whiskers doctor' is not Sick and care is have to Fido and that 'no an option. wellness imperative and helpful. However, consider their point of view.

It's bad enough going to the doctor when you are sick. It's worse going when you are well, only to be given a shot that makes you sick! Parents tell their children, "It will be okay, it's good for you!" But is it? What is in that shot? What is its purpose? Is it safe, efficacious, necessary, excessive? Should you be reassuring your fur kids, or should you be asking your veterinarian these important questions?

The first rule for being a good doctor is "Do no harm." I think during a first visit with a new client, and even each subsequent annual exam, there are six basic topics which should always be discussed, most importantly the utilization of products or procedures which could cause harm!

Following is a little list of topics you should be sure to discuss with your holistic-minded veterinarian:

* Vaccines/titer testing
* Medications (Heartworm preventatives, NSAID drugs)
* Pesticides (Flea and tick preventatives)
* Anesthetic/surgical episodes (spay, neuter procedures)
* Diet and Lifestyle
* Holistic modalities offered (acupuncture, essential oils)
* Reason for visit/main concern

Vaccination
What is its purpose?

I am *not* totally against vaccinations. But the medical breakthrough vaccines of yesteryear, which were designed to stop life threatening epidemics, are not the vaccines of today. Additionally many of the health breakthroughs were not due to vaccines, but rather major improvements in human hygiene and community sanitation. Unfortunately, the production and administration of today's vaccines are driven by greed and fear of lost income. I cover this topic first with you because many pet parents are still conditioned to take their pet to the vet because they get a notice that says a "shot is due". This should *not* be your main reason for a visit to the vet.

Dr. Ron Schultz, the infamous immunologist and researcher at the University of Wisconsin School of Veterinary Medicine has been heard to say, "The corona vaccine is a preventative in search of a disease." His meaning that, the existence of this product is quite unnecessary. It is certainly not what has been coined a core vaccine.

Dr. Schultz has been instrumental in establishing reduced vaccination protocols and the development of titer testing for our pet companions. It is his information that I have followed for many years with great success. He was my instructor in veterinary school. He has done work for many vaccine manufacturers and has been instrumental in the development of titer testing. He has reached out to veterinarians and pet guardians worldwide to educate about the truth of vaccinations and their impact on the immune system. He encouraged the AVMA to develop the concept of core vaccines, which has minimized the promotion of some vaccines by veterinarians.

So, if you ask yourself, why should I believe what Dr. Jodie says and not my current veterinarian? You can respectfully speak to your veterinarian and have the confidence knowing that the information that I present here comes to you with good authority, experience and research based on the world-renowned work of Dr. Ron Schultz! [1]

Vaccination

Is It Safe?

Every vaccination should be respected. Some say reactions are rare, but when your beloved little fur ball has a reaction, it doesn't feel so rare! Your kitty trusts you. Your new puppy has totally blind faith in your decision making. It is your job to educate yourself on the pros and cons of vaccinations. This is not a one size fits all cookie cutter program. A vaccination and titer testing plan should vary for every individual pet. You need to make informed decisions based on all the facts and options.

This is why your pet wants you to obtain the services of an integrative or holistic veterinary practitioner. A holistic vet has attended an accredited veterinary program (usually two to four years of undergraduate or pre-veterinary and then four years of veterinary school) just like a conventional or allopathic vet. Additionally, this holistic vet has attended seminars or read books about alternative and complementary ways to approach pet health care.

Most of us have at some point in our careers become open minded to the anecdotal reports and concerns voiced by clients and employees about problems with standard of care.

The internet has brought together many pet lovers who have had similar negative experiences with conventional preventatives and treatments. This accumulation of stories has made an impact and incited some change in the industry. Previously, these concerns were ignored as coincidental or rare. Today, social media is a buzz with the gripes and protests of pet parents who have become disillusioned with the status quo.

Fire's Story

Just a few months ago, I had a heart-to-heart discussion with an experienced veterinary technician who is now a groomer. She brings her dogs to see me periodically, and this visit was with a very special new purebred puppy. She had done a lot of research to obtain this little rising star. The prospect of giving this little guy a vaccination was not taken lightly by either of us. We both agreed that Fire would be living an at-risk lifestyle and so I gave him his DHPP complex vaccination.

A few days later, I received an emergency clinic report that Fire had been admitted and was fighting for his life! I called Fire's mom. She reported that he had a severe fever with swollen joints, and he could not walk. He couldn't even stand! She was really scared! He wouldn't eat and was getting weaker every day. He ended up spending a week in the emergency facility receiving intravenous fluids and other medications.

Ironically, even though I had administered the vaccination prior to the onset of this affliction, my colleagues at the emergency clinic, insisted that this malady could not have been caused by the vaccination. I insisted that it was.

For some reason, most veterinarians fail to acknowledge the basic rules, guidelines and explanations found in the vaccine manufacturers insert. I think it is important that *you* know what these are. Thankfully, Fire has recovered completely. His mom was diligent with prayer and a variety of detoxification protocols for vaccinosis.

Manufacturers have explained to me that a dog like Fire should never be vaccinated again, with anything, including rabies. Why? Different vaccines have common ingredients. Even though a vaccine may be stated as for a different disease, it could stimulate a similar reaction. We don't know what component caused Fire's near-death experience. What caused his high fever and all his joints to swell and even become temporarily deformed? This was scary! This is a good example of why it is important that states allow a veterinary exemption or waiver for the government mandated rabies vaccines. Think about Fire when you read the third warning, and feel comforted that he is now a handsome, gorgeous, happy, and alive dog!

* Vaccinate only *healthy* animals.
* Revaccination decisions should be made based on vet/client/patient relationship.
* Vaccines may produce anaphylaxis and/or inflammatory, immune-mediated hypersensitivity reactions.
* Tissue–origin vaccines contain extraneous protein that can lead to autoimmune disease.
* Vaccine may induce the development of injection-site fibrosarcoma (in cats).
* Maternal antibodies interfere with the development of immunity in a puppy or kitten.

Let us examine these a bit further. Let's pretend that YOU are a new client. Have a seat. I sit down on the floor with your pet, and we begin to talk. You tell me that your pet has been diagnosed with a thyroid disease.

As I review my new little patient's records, I ask, "Are your pet's vaccinations up-to-date?" "Oh, yes, is your reply, my other vet **just** took care of that!" This drives me crazy! This violates that number one recommendation in the manufacturer's insert! [2]

1. Vaccinate only healthy animals.

Surely everyone would agree patients afflicted with thyroid disease are **not** healthy! Yet, despite the manufacturer guidelines, the previous veterinarian administered vaccinations. I see this offense occur almost every day! One day the misdeed involves a hypothyroid dog, the next a hyperthyroid kitty. Commonly the crime is against an allergic pet or worse, a pet who has cancer! Yes, this happens! What is the justification for this? The client is often told that annual revaccination is a requirement. Yet, **manufacturer inserts say...**

2. Revaccination decisions should be made based on veterinarian/client/patient relationship.

What does this mean? The client gets to participate in the decision? Yes! In fact, in Wisconsin and many states, there is an informed consent law which **requires** the veterinarian to explain benefits and risks of every recommended procedure *before* implementation. What benefits and risks? Is there a benefit to giving a vaccination to a pet who is immune suppressed during allergy treatment with prednisone? No, the body cannot respond to a vaccination when it is immune suppressed. In fact, vaccine reactions are often suppressed intentionally, with prednisone treatment.

Does the risk of a reaction outweigh the need for the vaccine based on the pet's lifestyle? Commonly, the answer to this is, yes! Contrary to this, your former vet may have told you that annual revaccination is standard care and problems with vaccines are **un**common. Yet the **insert clearly says...**

3. **Vaccines may produce anaphylaxis and/or inflammatory, immune-mediated hypersensitivity reactions.**
4. **Tissue–origin vaccines contain extraneous protein that can lead to autoimmune disease.**

What is this all about? Manufacturers know that vaccines might not be safe? Vaccines might actually cause more harm than good? The manufacturer says the vaccine could cause autoimmune disease?

What is an example of an autoimmune disease? In humans, many are familiar with lupus. In pets, many are familiar with autoimmune hemolytic anemia (AIHA) or immune –mediated thrombocytopenia (IMTP). These are life-threatening blood disorders. Often, the cause is unidentified. In pets these disorders commonly occur within two weeks to three months after a vaccination.

There seems to be an epidemic of autoimmune thyroiditis in dogs, like Hashimoto's in humans. Paraphrasing Dr. Jean Dodd's, author of <u>Canine Thyroid Epidemic</u>, she explained that vaccines are known to stimulate autoimmunity and autoimmune destruction of the thyroid gland or its hormones. This leads to hypothyroidism. This gets passed on genetically. Thyroid disease is inherited.[3]

Thankfully, scientists are now affirming what many of us have known. If we eat and live unlike our parents, then the genes we received from them may *not* be expressed. This is the study of epigenetics and nutrigenomics. This is simply putting a fancy name and scientific validation to the idea, "Don't eat and act like your parents if you don't want to end up like them!" Of course, the converse is true as well. Researchers are now proposing autoimmune mechanisms as a cause for arthritis.[4] Concerned pet guardians cannot help but wonder about the vaccine connection to all this!

5. Vaccine may induce the development of injection-site fibrosarcomas (in cats).

What? The manufacturer says their vaccine might cause a malignant tumor? This is such a significant concern that veterinarians have been trained to administer this vaccine under the skin of the lower extremity, so if a tumor occurs, the leg can be amputated. Previously vaccines were commonly administered between the shoulder blades, if a tumor occurred, the mass would grow into the spine and there was little opportunity for successful removal. Isn't this a horrific solution?

My practice is inundated with the most chronically and severely ill patients because we offer alternatives for those pets for whom conventional approaches have failed. Many new clients have lost a pet to a vaccination problem. I always say, "When it is your pet that has a rare reaction, it doesn't feel so rare." It is particularly disheartening when you believe you were doing the right thing or a good thing and instead, your healthy pet was harmed. It is no surprise that loving pet parents become angry clients when they find out that they were not informed of the danger, nor were they told that their pet did not need a vaccination, which in the end caused harm.

My staff is always so excited when a fresh, new puppy or kitten arrives because we love nothing more than to get them off to a great start! We strive to provide a safe balance utilizing Western diagnostics and skills and Eastern thought and natural medicines.

Periodically, a savvy new pet guardian will say, "My regular vet told me those titers are a waste of money. The vaccine is cheaper and then you know your pet is protected. Just get the shot." But, now YOU, my new smart client might add to this discussion, "I had a friend whose puppy was vaccinated and died from parvo anyway." And you could cite #6.

Vaccination decisions are complicated. There is more to this decision than just doing what is least expensive! What the previous veterinarian did not explain is that it clearly states in the **vaccine manufacturer insert...**

6. **Maternal antibodies interfere with the development of immunity in a puppy (or kitten).**

If maternal antibodies block the effectiveness of the vaccine *and you do not know this*, then an exposed pup will get very ill, despite the injection having been administered. How can you know? Draw some blood and check a titer! A titer measures the development of immunity.

Why do vaccine manufacturers make these statements and place them inside every vaccine package? They do not wish to be held liable for harm which may occur due to the improper utilization of their product. For this same reason, veterinary advisors who work for these companies will recommend that vaccines **not** be repeated after a one-time reaction.

What? My clients tell me their reactive pets simply receive an antihistamine injection every year prior to the administration of the offending vaccine. **If a vaccine administration is ill-advised by the manufacturer, who becomes liable? The veterinarian is now at fault for ignoring the warning.**

Do you feel like, "I am so confused; I just want to do what is best?" Be your pet's advocate. Now you know that it is okay to at least question the routine administration of vaccinations.

In many states, a legal rabies waiver can be provided for ill pets.

A DHPP (for dogs) or a DRC (for cats) should not be given at all if a pet has an illness. Examples of illness are cancer, allergies, diabetes, hypothyroidism, hyperthyroidism, Cushings, Addison's and many more imbalances or types of dis-ease.

Titer testing is a scientific, objective aid to the decision-making whether vaccination is necessary for patient protection.

What Is a Titer?
Why Should You Measure One?

Titer is correctly spelled titre or titer. It is pronounced tight-er. It is a blood test which measures the immune response to an antigen exposure. The number measured is an antibody level present at different titration or dilution levels of the blood. The antigen that the body has been exposed to, to stimulate the immune response, could have been present in a vaccination or the disease itself.

If antibody levels are present in highly diluted blood, then that is a high titer. A high titer level may indicate lots of exposure, lots of protection or perhaps long-lasting immunity. The titer level is one indicator of the body's immune response to an antigenic stimulation.

A lot of research has been performed on dog and cat serum to establish what antibody titer levels are protective against distemper/parvo and distemper/rhino/calici respectively. Comparable research does NOT exist to assert what titer levels are protective against the rabies virus. Challenge studies based on time interval since last vaccination have been performed for rabies. This is what dictates the 1-year initial, 3-year booster rule. There is an ongoing study to try to prove the 3- year vaccine for rabies actually protects for 7 years.

It is useful to understand that the titer measures antibody levels in the blood which is part of the body's humoral defense system. In addition to this protection, our body has a cellular defense. This is at the mucous lining level. A body can stop an offending antigen as it enters your nasal passage or mouth for example, before it enters the bloodstream. This protection is NOT measured by a titer. So, if your pet has a low titer, that may increase his susceptibility to disease, but his cellular immunity could still afford him all the necessary protection.

Within the humoral defense are two levels: sterilizing immunity and memory immunity. If your pet has a high number of antibodies in the blood, it may be a sterilizing level. This means if he is exposed to the disease, his body will neutralize it so easily, you will not even know he was exposed! If your pet has a low level of antibodies in the blood, it may be a memory level. This means if he is exposed to the disease, he may become somewhat ill, but will 'remember', fight and overcome the disease.

Therefore, you should realize it is your pet's immune *response to* a vaccination, NOT the vaccination itself that protects your pet from disease. There exists the phenomenon of no responders and low responders. Some pets simply don't respond to vaccination. Some pets, even with repetitive vaccinations are low responders. It is important to be aware if your pet is a poor responder. You would not want to assume that just because your pet has been vaccinated that he is protected. Many dog enthusiasts have heard of someone who has lost a pet to parvo even though the dog was vaccinated.

There are many reasons for vaccination failure. A titer is a blood draw that serves as one tool to assure you that your pet companion is protected. Titer levels and recommendations based on them should be very individualized. A pet's lifestyle should be considered when making titer or vaccination recommendations. If your pet has a high titer, he does not need to be vaccinated with that antigen. If he has a low titer despite a history of lots of exposure to that antigen, then another vaccination is not going to boost him any further. In fact, repeating an unnecessary or ineffective vaccination could be harmful.

Vaccines have been associated with vomiting, diarrhea, fevers, rashes, anaphylaxis, vaccine site tumors, seizures and immune mediated disorders. A veterinarian who is experienced with utilizing titre information can provide you with guidance as to when to perform a titer and then based on that result, whether to boost.

I recommend vaccinating puppies with distemper/hepatitis/parainfluenza/parvo at 8 and 12 weeks. Do an in-clinic or rapid result titer at 16 to 20 weeks.

It measures only distemper and parvo (sometimes hepatitis). If it is positive for both, then this means there is a sterilizing level of protection. I then give the rabies vaccine. If one or the other is negative, there could still be adequate memory or even cellular immunity, however in a puppy who has not been "over vaccinated", who has not had any reaction, and who could have had mother's antibody present at time of prior vaccination, blocking the effectiveness of the vaccine, I would boost again with whichever individual vaccine was needed.

It is of notable interest that in hundreds of puppies/dogs on whom we performed hepatitis/adenovirus titer testing not one was unprotected. Therefore, we no longer test for this antibody level. At the dog's annual wellness exam, we perform a titer which delivers actual number results. This takes two weeks. These results tell me if the pet's prior vaccinations have stimulated the pet's immune system to a degree that he has either memory or sterilizing immunity levels. I decide based on the pet's age, lifestyle, other disorders present, previous number of vaccines, guardian's concerns about vaccine reactions, whether a booster is recommended. If you are my client, I will email you to report the results and give a recommendation.

The most a titer drops in one year is in half. So, depending on how high it starts the first time we check it, we can extrapolate and tell a client, a doggy day care, a boarding kennel, how often we feel a titer needs to be checked on an individual to assure that he is protected. Some dogs are checked annually to satisfy a kennel requirement, others have NOT been checked NOR vaccinated for several years and then have still been found to have protective levels. Obviously, this saves the pet a lot of vaccine-associated risk and saves you, the client a lot of money!

Sometimes a new client whose pet has been vaccinated annually for many years receives his first titer test when older. Despite all that vaccine we determine he's a low responder. This tells us to stop vaccinating! The client has been wasting money and taking unnecessary risk with his pet's immune health. That pet needs to be careful where he goes, what he sniffs, and what he eats (i.e. other dog poo).

Specific **canine titer parameters** are as follows:
Michigan State University reports:

CDV≥ 32   CPV≥ 80
(Distemper)   (Parvo)
These levels would be considered protective, roughly equivalent to **sterilizing** immunity.

Dr. Ron Schultz at the University of Wisconsin-Madison VMTH has explained that his research shows:
CDV≥ 4   CPV≥ 20

These levels may also be protective, but roughly equivalent to **memory** levels of immunity.

Specific **feline titer parameters** are as follows:

Michigan State "sterilizing" levels:

CIV≥ 32   FVR≥ 16   FPV≥ 40
(Calici)   (Herpes/Rhino)   (Distemper/Panleuk)

Dr. Ron Schultz at the UW-Madison VMTH has explained that his research shows "memory levels":

CIV≥ 4   FVR≥ 2   FPV≥ 8

Rabies Vaccine, Titer or Waiver?

All states require rabies vaccines for dogs, this is *not* necessarily so for cats. Efficacy and legal guidelines for administration of rabies vaccine is based on duration of immunity to challenge studies, *not* on titer levels. Therefore, performance of titer testing for rabies protection does not yield usable results legally. Currently, these can be run at Kansas State. Keep in mind, vaccine manufacturers state that a vaccine should only be administered to "healthy dogs and cats." Efficacy could be affected by "stress, weather, nutrition, disease, parasitism, concurrent treatments, individual idiosyncrasies or impaired immunological competency." **Therefore, the administration of a vaccine does not guarantee protection.** Unfortunately, only a few states allow rabies waivers. You do *not* need to give your pets any other vaccines by law.

Ask questions before you consent to the vaccination of a pet, especially if they live an isolated life, have allergies, diabetes, otitis, parasites, hypothyroidism, epilepsy, kidney disease, hyperadrenocorticism, cancer or other disease.

Avoid Products and Medications

With Side Effects

Most veterinarians are trained to discuss and recommend heartworm preventatives and flea and tick preventatives at your first visit and almost every visit thereafter. Additionally, they have very limited tools in their toolboxes. So, if a pet has any amount of inflammation, conventional vets often prescribe antibiotics and/or steroids or non-steroidals.

I am an options vet. I believe in telling you the pros and cons of everything to the best of my ability. In many states, there is an informed consent law which requires just that. A veterinarian by law is required to tell you all your options including potential benefits and risks. However, guess what? It is legal to leave out "alternative" care options. So, I am here to fill you in on those. You might want to know.

Let us cover a brief synopsis of the pros, cons and alternatives for the big five:

* Heartworm preventatives
* Flea and tick products
* Antibiotics
* Steroids/glucocorticoids/cortisone/prednisone
* Non-steroidals/NSAIDs

I am a conventionally trained and holistically trained veterinarian. I consider myself integrative. I have used all of these products in my practice when necessary. There are some good reasons to use allopathic medications, but there are many reasons to try to avoid them.

East meets West

Several years ago, I was fortunate to be able to take an acupuncture class "field trip" to China. A family member accompanied me. We traveled with my instructor, the world renown, Dr. Huisheng Xie. The plan was to spend the first half of the trip listening to academic presentations in Shanghai and the second half traveling to remote areas to experience true China. We would pack up our belongings and ride across the country on camels to visit a Shaolin temple and see the Great Wall. Sliding down the dunes on inner tubes would even be included!

We enjoyed the presentations and the French cuisine in the New York style Shanghai hotel. Next, we were treated to authentic Chinese faire at a fancy restaurant in the small million-person town of Lanzhou. My family member and I are vegetarians. We expected to survive on rice, but much to our dismay, rice was not a staple food in these Chinese restaurants.

The body parts and foreign vegetables presented on the beautiful clear glass lazy Susan table were not appealing to the palates of these two Midwestern girls. My poor traveling companion does eat some fish, so she decided to try the mysterious broth in the Golden Urn. At first, her tummy upset was met with some herbal tea prescribed by the Chinese American doctor in our group.

Next, there was the fun usage of this poor sick girl for an acupuncture demonstration, performed by personnel in a Chinese military teaching hospital. She was selected to see if this treatment would help make her feel better. Little did I know that what was in that bowl would cause fear in me like none other. It was the only item that she consumed differently from me.

As the evening proceeded, she became progressively ill. It culminated with a fever of 106 and a diagnosis of dysentery made by a non-English speaking doctor in a horrific Chinese hospital. Our travel group left us behind as they went on to ride the camels and climb the Great Wall. We were only accompanied by two non-English speaking veterinary students who held electronic language interpreters. It was the middle of the night and the military hospital would not allow us in. The students were upset that we had to go to the other hospital. I found out why.

No one spoke English. There was one bathroom with one sink with cold water, no soap, only a trough and no lights. Good thing! The bathroom odor and sound of the trickling trough told me I did not need a visual. Old, robed men were lying on rusted, blood-stained gurneys in the hallway. There were visible cockroaches climbing in and out of the cabinet in the treatment room. I had to slap off blood-filled mosquitoes while we were there. Thank goodness, this illness caused her to be unconscious most of the time!

She almost died. But, after two intravenous catheters were placed to deliver life-saving fluids for severe dehydration, and antibiotics were administered for septicemia, we completed twelve excruciating hours of praying for survival and then left as quickly as we had arrived, for fear that she would contract some other contagion!

I was immensely grateful for the Chinese doctor's ability to deliver this allopathic care that saved the life of my family member. I learned that savvy world travelers carry ciprofloxacin in their carry-on luggage!

My point here is that there is a time and place for Western and Eastern medical approaches. It is wonderful to be aware of the benefits and risks of each and to be able to have access to both types of medical care. Integration of these can be the ideal approach for many patients, furry or not!

Heartworm Preventatives

So, here is my take on heartworm prevention. The fear of this disease will vary depending on where you live and your pet's lifestyle. There are certainly some patients who do not need preventative medicine.

You need to assess your pet's exposure to mosquitoes and the saturation of dogs in the community. Dog contact is not needed. A mosquito can bite a neighbor dog and fly over the fence into your yard and transmit the heartworm larvae.

Cats are naturally resistant to heartworm. Cats who are immune suppressed like those with feline leukemia or FIV (Feline Immunosuppressive Virus) are susceptible, as are humans with HIV/AIDS.

Some guardians believe that if their pets are fed properly and live stress-free lives, they will not contract disease. I like to believe that there is a lot of truth to that. However, stress happens!

Ebony's Story

I recall one loving pet mom who was quite distraught when her 6-year-old black lab came up positive on her heartworm screening test. She was a raw feeder and her dogs always participated in fabulous exercise. She did not believe in using heartworm preventatives.

When informed of the positive test, Mom said, "Ooh, I know what happened, we are moving, and it has been very stressful for the dogs." This woman was hard core into natural medicine. So, even with this diagnosis, she wanted to avoid conventional treatment. This was many years ago, early in my holistic career. She coerced me into researching an all herbal treatment. I did. We used it and after almost two years, the dog's heartworm status converted to negative. The dog had no side effects and no decreased quality of life during that treatment time. We were all incredibly pleased.

This is also the time frame that it takes for a single worm to die naturally. It is possible to be infested with many adult worms, a single adult worm or worms of all one sex. If there is a female present that can produce babies, then these babies are called microfilaria.

The heartworm life cycle is a complicated parasite life cycle due to multiple larval stages. However, if you can understand the life cycle then you can make a very informed decision as to how you want to prevent or treat heartworm. This is not a one-size fits all decision.

I counsel my clients to think about it this way. Heartworm preventative is a de-wormer. It kills parasites which are contracted during the month prior, in fact, 45 days prior. Most oral brands de-worm the heartworm which is contracted from mosquito exposure and the same pill de-worms for intestinal parasites which come from ingesting fecal matter or little outdoor critters such as mice, rabbits, or chipmunks.

You can help decide your pet's risk. Does your dog stay indoors most of the time? Do you live on a lake? Does your dog help you garden in the evening? Are you a snowbird? Do you take your dog with you down south or do you live in a warm, humid country-side year-round?

Your answers to these questions can help determine if you should give this medication seasonally or year-round. A June 1 pill will de-worm all the way back to the middle of April, so it is not necessary to give an April 1 heartworm pill in Wisconsin unless you are concerned about exposure to intestinal worms. Keep in mind a November 1 pill takes care of October, not November.

If you choose to prevent seasonally or not at all, then it is especially important to test for heartworm every spring. It takes five months to show up on a blood test. It makes no sense to test in the fall, as heartworm contracted that summer will not show up on the test. If you are giving monthly medication year-round, then you can test any time of year. The purpose of this is to catch the disease early if you missed a pill or if your pet expelled it without you knowing.

There are also some breeds (ex. Collies) which have the MDR1 gene which makes them particularly sensitive to ivermectin. Several brands contain this. There is a blood test to check for this sensitivity. A brand which contains milbemycin could be used instead. Some holistic pet guardians prefer one brand over the other. Some believe there may be less liver enzyme elevation, but I have not seen that to be necessarily true. Both drugs are metabolized by the liver.

If you would like to help drug removal along you can provide some oral liver detox herbals for several days to one week after the pill is given. In my practice, I recommend a safe and effective glycerin extract formulated by Greg Tilford, an herbalist that I trust, which contains milk thistle and burdock root, two great liver cleansers! This recommendation is one small touch that separates a holistic from a conventional practitioner.

I also strongly suggest that you do your best to question the 'inactive' ingredients in medications that you choose. Chewables and especially soft chews can contain some appalling ingredients. Here is an example of what inactive ingredients can cause.

Edgar's Story

Years ago, I had a client who swore her Golden Retriever was allergic to his heartworm preventative. Every spring when she administered this medication, he became severely itchy. He was miserable with puffy eyes and hot spots. In the winter, his pruritus went away. I thought it was an environmental, summer allergy. (This experience was before I became a holistic detective!)

I knew the drug was metabolized by the liver and gone in a day. I did not think about the longer-term food allergy impact of the inactive flavoring in the medication. Also, we were never told what the inactive ingredients were, until this year (2016)! I was shocked! I swear they chose the fifteen worst ingredients they could think of and put them into this product. I have discontinued this product in my practice.

Years ago, that Golden Retriever's guardian had the sense to discontinue the medication. She said she would take her chances with heartworm disease, as at the time, there was no other alternative preventative. That dog's "allergies" went away when the medication was discontinued.

The inactive ingredients in that product are: *beef, soy flour, meat by-products, sugar, gelatin, tapioca starch, wheat gluten, propylene glycol, phosphoric acid, salt, garlic powder, brewer's yeast, onion powder, dried cheddar cheese, potassium sorbate, caramel color, natural smoke flavor, mixed tocopherols, FD&C red#40.* Can you spot any potential allergens, toxins, or inflammatory agents? You don't have enough fingers to count them all!

Flea and Tick Products

Please avoid the spot-ons and the oral pesticide preventatives. Many, especially the permethrins, have been shown to be carcinogenic. Many guardians report damage to skin locally and neurologic symptoms or lethargy after application. In most cases, the insect needs to bite the pet and potentially transmit disease before the pest is killed by the product anyway. These products are absorbed into the lipid layer and blood stream of the pet and are cumulative. They are not cleared in a day, the way we discussed occurs with a heart worm preventative. (More on this in Chapter 7.)

Here again, essential oils to the rescue. I have formulated a blend of essential oils which I have recommended and sold with great success for over a decade. No preventative is 100% effective, but I have been pleased with the feedback that I have received on the safety and efficacy of my 100% essential oil spray. I promote it as a summer coat spray, but it does contain all-natural chemical constituents which have been shown to have insect repellant properties.

My clients have compared it to their prior experiences using spot-ons. To deter even tough insects, such as ticks, their re-purchase tells me that these quality oils work.
You can formulate a DIY blend, or you can purchase my tried and proven product. In either case, you will be providing great service for your pet by avoiding the synthetic chemicals in the conventional pesticides sold by vets and in pet retail shops or even tractor supply stores.

These essential oils are healthy for you too. So, you can spray these on your hands to carefully apply these to your pet's ears and face.

I am more concerned about you and your pet's exposure to cancer causing pesticides and the prevalence of cancer in our pets, than I am the off chance of flea or tick exposure. We must begin to weigh our concern about a nuisance issue vs. the detriment from exposure to an adverse treatment.

This leads us to discuss the next three drug categories: antibiotics, steroids, and NSAIDs (non-steroidal anti-inflammatory drugs. How does the "Good Vet, the Integrative Vet" that your pet desires, handle these topics?

Antibiotics

Antibiotics have their time of need in health care, but they have been abused and they are currently the cause of a lot of morbidity and mortality in our human hospitals, and much of the chronic gastrointestinal issues, chronic skin problems and more in our pets today. They are often a quick way out for a doctor, honestly, to get you out of the office! This is a crime!

Early in my veterinary career, I was taught by other practitioners that if you did not know what was wrong, just do the "shotgun" approach.
Prescribe antibiotics and steroids. If there is infection, the antibiotic will take care of it. If there is painful inflammation, the steroid will take care of that. Aagh! That's a terrible plan.

Overuse of antibiotics for viral conditions, for mild bacterial infections, and as feed additives for our livestock to promote growth, has led to serious antibiotic resistance in our world.

Sharday's Story

A sad story with a great happy ending is about a pit bull who was mangled by another dog. Care was delayed due to lack of finances. The emergency clinic told the distraught guardian that the dog's foreleg would need to be amputated. This dog presented to my practice dejected in spirit, severely swollen with skin flaps hanging and full of debris. Closing wounds was not a good idea medically and not feasible financially.

So, on a zero budget we began soaking this dog and these wounds in a full body bath with Nature Rich soap, essential oils and then following with a topical Chinese herbal applied into the wounds. My techs loved on this girl and soaked her faithfully in the hospital every day.
She received probiotics, great natural food and herbal analgesics. She healed miraculously. She kept her leg and today, probably five years later, she continues to live a quality life, virtually scar free. She never received any surgery, no antibiotics. The body can do amazing things when given the chance.

Always use probiotics with antibiotics, and many times, you can use probiotics in place of antibiotics. Probiotics have been discussed at length in other chapters.

Steroids

Just like the "shotgun" approach, I also had subscribed to the notion that you should not let anyone die without the benefit of steroids. Unless of course they are in a healing crisis, then steroids could stop that whole process! A healing crisis is scary but can result in a miracle. Suppressing the body's immune system with steroids is rarely a good idea.

Steroids go by several names: glucocorticoids, prednisone, prednisolone, dexamethasone, cortisone, hydrocortisone, methylprednisolone and many more. Please beware that if your pet is *taken in the back* by the technician, he may receive a steroid injection against your wishes. In Wisconsin, this violates the informed consent law. It is still common for an injection of this nature to be called an "allergy shot". It is not!

The phrase allergy shots should only include hyposensitization injections, not short or long-acting steroid injections. Steroid injections will stop almost any itch and make almost any discomfort go away, but, at what cost?

Side effects include excessive thirst and urine volumes which can make a lake of your kitchen floor. This medication suppresses the immune system to such a degree that your pet can develop ear infections, skin infections, bladder infections and more. It can cause GI ulceration and should NEVER be combined with an NSAID (including aspirin), nor given when your pet might be dehydrated. Long term steroid use weakens ligaments. Think torn cruciate ligaments, hmmm. Steroid use can cause iatrogenic (doctor induced) Cushings disease.[5]

Koby's Story

Let me tell you about Koby. This sweet, neutered, male Golden Retriever presented to me at only 1 ½ years of age with a severe case of iatrogenic (doctor induced) Cushing's disease. He had been treated with strong immunosuppressive drugs, including steroids for almost his entire life. The university was managing him for an incurable autoimmune disease peculiar to Goldens called masticatory myositis. Koby was unable to open his mouth. His head and jaw muscles had atrophied. He could no longer carry a tennis ball and he could barely eat, despite this strong treatment.

Side effects from the steroids were causing him to urinate in the house. He had a giant pot belly, a very sparse coat and a tragic old dog expression. He had developed multiple hard, stone-like accumulations under his skin called calcinosis cutis.

His guardian said she would try anything I suggested or put Koby to sleep. They were both sadly miserable. **I had never seen this rare condition before, but I believe that given the right nutritional tools and a lot of positive thought, the body can heal itself from almost any affliction.**

We began an exclusive, balanced, high-pressure pasteurized raw meat diet. No starch. No synthetics. No vaccinations. We used a gut health/liver detox/immune supportive whole food supplement/herbal program! We very gradually weaned off the prednisone. Koby began to slowly improve. In less than one year he had completely recovered!

He recovered from the horrific steroid side effects and his incurable disorder was gone! All his skeletal muscle and masticatory function returned. Now, it has been three years since we began Koby's care, and he continues to be 100% normal. He is gorgeous and strong and loves his tennis ball. He has one calcified lesion under the skin of his right shoulder. It is a bit of a souvenir to remind us of the miracle that he is!

NSAIDs
(Non-steroidal anti-inflammatory drugs)

NSAIDs do not suppress the immune system in the same manner as steroids, but they do suppress inflammation. Inflammation can be uncomfortable, but it is the body's foremost healing mechanism. When your pet gets a cut, it immediately becomes inflamed. The swelling and redness is the increase in circulation that is bringing the healing cells to the affected location. Too often we view inflammation as a bad thing that needs to be suppressed. Suppressing this normal function can delay healing.[6]

Selecting a veterinarian who is willing to let nature take its course, assist the body to heal in a gentle natural way and not suppress normal bodily functions, is a step in the right direction toward living with your pet's nature in mind.

Some NSAID names with which you might be familiar are: carpofen (Rimadyl®), meloxicam (Metacam®), etodolac (Etogesic®), firocoxib (Previcox®), deracoxib, (Deramaxx®)

These are in the ibuprofen (Advil®) family. Ibuprofen should never be given to dogs or cats as it can certainly cause kidney failure. Some of these veterinary products damage dog kidneys as well and are completely unsafe for cats.[7]

All NSAIDs can cause stomach upset with potential ulceration[8] and most, including aspirin, damage cartilage over time![9,10] Cartilage is the cushioning in the joint that we want to protect for joint comfort and function!

Some of these have caused liver disease, kidney disease, dry eye, gastrointestinal (GI) ulceration and even death.

Additionally, aspirin decreases platelet function. This prevents clotting. Many people say it "thins the blood". Therefore, it is used with cardiovascular disease to prevent clots or strokes.

It is for this rare anti-clotting reason that we do periodically prescribe aspirin for cats, although it is typically considered to be toxic in this species. Be sure to tell your vet if you are giving aspirin to your pet. Some clients keep this a secret. Then, when their pet has a simple procedure, like a tooth extraction, they wonder why the pet is unable to stop bleeding. This is a serious side effect of aspirin. Although, it too, can decrease or eliminate pain, aspirin also damages cartilage over time. Choosing cheap can be dangerous.

As an integrative practitioner, I add a natural GI protectant when I prescribe an NSAID. This may be a zinc product or a delicious, clear, sticky mushroom complex (Alicaid™), designed to prevent GI ulcers.

There are many natural alternatives to the NSAIDs. I dispense a lot of **corydalis**! This Chinese herb is anti-inflammatory and analgesic. It can decrease swelling and pain perception. Other than an aversion to the taste or loose stool if given too much, I have seen no side effects, even using this long term in my practice.

Since I began using the economical powder version at least 15 years ago, I have seen the advent of many natural, herbal commercial brands for humans and pets, which incorporate corydalis into their tablet or capsule blend. Some of these products also contain anti-inflammatory **boswellia** species or analgesic and mildly sedating **California poppy.**

Essential Oils for Pets

Of course, we can also assist our pets with discomfort, skin, and immune support by using essential oils in a diffuser, topically and even orally if we are careful. Some of these oils are frankincense, copaiba, wintergreen, clove and peppermint.

Frankincense, Copaiba, Panaway™

Frankincense contains boswellic acids, copaiba is high in beta-caryophyllene, wintergreen contains salicylates (the active components in aspirin), clove creates a numbing sensation and peppermint provides a deep warm/cool penetration. Helichrysum supports a healthy cardiovascular system and is often applied safely over bruised tissues.[11, 12]

A holistic vet experienced in using safe and effective essential oils can really help you use these oils properly in your pet. Doing an oils massage demo is one of my favorite doctor patient activities!

Contact a veterinarian experienced with the use of essential oils in dogs and cats to help you choose a brand that is safe and effective for pets.

Organ Removal? Unique Holistic Perspective

Do you remember watching the first release of Planet of the Apes? Any chance you thought of your pet when you watched the apes force castration upon the humans to make them more docile? Is this what God meant when he told Adam, "Thou shalt have dominion over the beasts of the Earth?" Is this good stewardship?

It has long been accepted to sterilize our pets to control over population. As veterinarians, we were taught to counsel clients that it was in their pets' best interests to spay their females to prevent mammary cancer and to neuter their males to prevent aggression and prostate disease.

Recent studies are now showing that these procedures are not necessarily in the best interests of your dog or cat. Indeed, in large breed dogs, there is a correlation between neutering and an increased incidence of bone disorders, such as osteosarcoma, a serious bone cancer.[13] Many pet families suffer with the mess of a spayed female dog becoming urinary incontinent because her ovaries were removed.

As times change and more information becomes available, you will want to make an informed decision if and when you want to have any type of spay or neuter procedure performed on your pet. Are you 'living with your pet in mind' if you have these procedures done, or are you conforming to a societal expectation?

Retrospective studies are just becoming available which show that the early age spay or neuter procedure being performed through humane societies and shelters, before you even obtain your pet, is not in the long-term best interest of your dog or cat. I warned of this many years ago and unfortunately my fears have become justified.

I understand the concern voiced by those who must witness pet overpopulation on the front lines. I too have worked in a humane society and was responsible for performing mass euthanasia. However, what we have learned is our current approach is not solving that problem. In other countries where castration and ovariohysterectomy is NOT routine, pet guardians may be more responsible and ironically there is no population problem.

In America, the dirty hidden secret behind pet overpopulation begins with the puppy mill deception. Cruel breeders are pumping out puppies from cage bound dogs and then shipping them to pet shops, flea market vendors and even shelters, claiming that these are strays and their "shelter" is full. They say these pets will be euthanized if another shelter does not help and take them. A lot of money is paid for these pets that are "vetted" and ready to go.

Intentional puppy mill-sourced pups are farmed out to sellers, where the claim is made to you, the buyer, that the pup was locally born. However, there is never a mother or father anywhere to be seen. In fact, many of these sellers, posing as breeders, meet the prospective buyer at a wayside or parking lot claiming they don't want strangers in the home due to disease.

I think the solution is a moratorium on all pet breeding. Levy stiff fines and jail time. If we really want to live with our pets in mind, then we need to stop perpetuating this problem. I have talked to many pet parents who purchased their dog from what they knew originated as a puppy mill situation, but said, "I didn't know what to do, I wanted to help them, and get them out of there."

Because of all this deception, responsible pet guardians continue to spay and neuter their pets, who never leave the yard, thinking it is their moral obligation, even though they are jeopardizing their own family member's health.[14, 15, 16]

Be aware that you also have the surgical option to allow your female pet to keep her ovaries but remove her uterus. This is a hysterectomy, not an ovariohysterectomy. Male dogs can have a vasectomy. These procedures will maintain hormone function but prevent pregnancy. They will also allow some of the objectionable behaviors to occur for which many guardians seek sterilization in the first place, such as aggressive tendencies or running away. Many neutered male dogs still lift their leg inappropriately. An organ removal surgery is no guarantee that you will be able to prevent an objectionable behavior.

Most veterinarians have not been taught how to perform these alternative procedures. Watch for the development of these skills and alternative recommendations in the future as a new awareness spreads though out the pet and veterinary industry.

If your pet no longer has these organs, you could consider a glandular support. I actually formulate a product which contains pork uterus, kidney and cordyceps mushroom to support urinary tract health. It is called P-Support! There are several whole food and glandular companies that produce products to fill this void. Consider Standard Process® Symplex F or M.

Acupuncture
What Does Your Pet Think About Acupuncture?

Acupuncture is a modality commonly associated with holistic care. Many of us believe a good integrative vet would be providing a wonderful, beneficial service for your cat or dog if the condition indicated that acupuncture might be a treatment of choice.

I became certified in 2008, by the Chi Institute to practice acupuncture on animals, with the intent that it would help alleviate pain and even manage some metabolic disorders.

I quickly learned that acupuncture was ideal for musculoskeletal disease management. There are many orthopedic problems that are managed better with acupuncture, than with any other modality.

In my experience, disc disease responds very well to acupuncture. In fact, with surgery, there is a risk of thermal injury to the spinal cord. So, if a little dachshund is developing rear limb paralysis due to bulging disc pressure on the spinal cord, surgery might cause an ascending paralysis and leave this little guy paralyzed in the front end as well.

Indeed, this is true. I saw a Basset Hound for acupuncture treatment. I was contacted after a university surgical intervention caused this patient's rear limb paresis (weakness) to progress to front limb paralysis. Unfortunately, this scenario ended with euthanasia.

111

Most people cannot handle the emotional and physical difficulties associated with caring for a quadriplegic dog. If I had been able to intervene sooner, I might have been able to get this guy walking again or at worst he could have lived a very satisfying life in a cart, using a pre-surgery, strong, front end. You can see many great videos online of dogs having fun in their carts!

But this leads me to a topic that I think is rarely addressed, would your pet *like* acupuncture? What do pets think about this idea? Many people are mortified at the idea of someone sticking multiple needles into them! If our pets had a choice, if they could talk, what would they say? I have developed my own impressions, but I decided to ask some animal communicators.

Missy's Story

Asia Voight is an internationally known animal communicator, intuitive life guide, teacher, inspirational speaker, radio host and author. Asia connects with animals on a soul level to help resolve emotional and behavioral issues while assisting in deepening their bond with their human companions. She has assisted over 80,000 animal and human clients. I asked Asia if any of her pet clients told her how they feel about the acupuncture procedure.

This was her response,

My client, Vicki, fretted over her dog, Missy, a gangly German Shepherd mix. Missy had been a wild pup rescued from a barn. Years later, she still barely tolerated the softest of touches from strangers. Missy suffered from a bowel disorder. The medicine from her vet made Missy's colon convulse, even bleed. Vicki had to try something; she could not bear to watch Missy suffer. She thought to try acupuncture.

This though would entail someone touching Missy, not only with a hand, but also with needles! Vicki had found personal relief from stomach pain with acupuncture, so she was sure this modality would help her fur child. If only she could get Missy's permission and understanding. She hired me to convince Missy to hold still instead of running from strangers and give acupuncture a chance! This is how the communication session proceeded...

"Hello Missy, nice to meet you. I'm invited here to communicate with you about a new treatment for your aching body. Can I share this information with you?" Missy physically tilted her head in a curious manner, along with sending me an energetic open-heart sensation. "The treatment is called acupuncture. It entails a different kind of veterinarian placing tiny needles into your body so the energy can flow correctly and heal you. Will you agree to give this a try? You will need to hold very still." Missy scanned into my mind. She could see I had also tried acupuncture and that I was relaxed during the process. Missy lifted her head looking at Vicki with soft eyes, the deal was set.

A few days later Connie, the acupuncturist, came over to Vicki's home and slowly walked up to Missy. Missy sat quietly in the living room and fell over onto her side when Connie approached! Vicki watched on, with her hand over her mouth. She had never seen Missy respond this way to anyone but her. The needles were carefully placed; Missy let out a sigh and was soon snoring!

The next day Asia checked in with Missy again, this is what Missy told her, *"I let go of all worry when I could feel the needles working to heal and relax me. It wasn't hard or scary. I know I will get better now."*

As a veterinary acupuncturist, I have observed a difference in the behavior of acupuncture patients when they are told what to expect, when they are prepped by a confident guardian and when they come back a second time and have learned for themselves that all will be well!

Murphy's Thoughts

Carolee Biddle, a popular Milwaukee, Wisconsin area animal communicator shared this incite:

Our dog, Murphy, received acupuncture treatments to manage her pain from elbow dysplasia. Murphy said, "It sends me into la-la land!" She would sleep all day after a treatment and then be extra perky the next!

I can't remember any dogs saying they did not like an acupuncture treatment. Some dogs didn't like the electrical stimulus hooked up to the needles. They told me, "It is too strong, too much, an energy overload."

Acupuncture stimulates the body at nerve junctions causing an endorphin release, our euphoric hormone! This is one of the major reasons why people and pets enjoy acupuncture.

Electrostimulation with needles, much like a TENS unit, can be excitatory or numbing. It is difficult to provide this properly for animals as we cannot get their immediate or direct feedback as to how the procedure feels. This variation of acupuncture can be immensely helpful for paralysis, but should never be used on pets with seizure disorders. I appreciate the feedback from animal communicators on this particular topic.

My experiences with acupuncture treatments have also shown me that many dogs or cats are, initially, very receptive to treatments when they know they need them. When they are better, they often indicate they no longer want the treatment.

The indicators can be subtle or dramatic. Some of my patients will begin to get antsy or wiggle away. I need to be receptive and listen to that. I have had a couple of patients try to bite me. One terrier lunged unexpectedly and forced me against the wall.

Acupuncture should be a pleasant experience, and for most it is abundantly pleasurable! All doctors have different styles and so-called bed side manners. I do not believe in forcing acupuncture upon my patients. I have seen some acupuncturists expect a pet parent to hold down their dog or cat, or even apply a muzzle. I avoid this.

It is important that an acupuncturist enter the procedure with good intent. I explain what we are going to do and often combine my initial touches with some massage techniques and essential oils. We always work on the floor; the room is dimly lit and meditative music plays. This ambiance not only relaxes the patient and pet parent, but also helps me to focus.

Kitties Love Acupuncture!

My favorite anecdote is a story that validates how pets can decide for themselves what they enjoy and what is good for them. Two ancient grandma kitties make me smile just thinking about their attitude toward acupuncture. The hallway to my acupuncture room is about thirty feet, a long walk for cats in their twenties! When each of these kitties arrived, we would let them out of their carriers at the far extent of that long hallway to observe their mobility. They were both visiting to receive acupuncture for severe arthritis.

Each visit we let them out, they walked a few inches, cats rarely cooperate, and then they were carried the rest of the way to the acupuncture room. As they become aware of the location of the acupuncture room and the experience that transpired there, they would say, "I can make it on my own." And then proceed to strut their stuff, down the long corridor, making a correct turn into the cozy acupuncture room, avoiding the opposite turn to the conventional exam room. There they would investigate the room and quickly settle in, onto the blanket or pillow provided as if to say, "Let's get to it, I know this treatment will feel great!"

This made my day. It was always a highlight to laugh, as we watched them make their way down that long hall, to that special room, with their own motivation.

I believe the pet knows if my focus is on his or her healing. I enjoy answering questions, but during an acupuncture treatment it is best to keep chit-chat to a minimum. This mindedness is important with all energy healing modalities.

Pet behavior will commonly help guide doctor and pet parent in the decision as to frequency of treatments. Studies have shown that acupuncture efficacy takes off after approximately four treatments. If it does not, then it may not be the best modality choice for your pet.

If your pet's condition has become severe and chronic, it may be unreasonable to expect acupuncture to heal the condition. However, acupuncture is a great modality to improve quality of life without any adverse side effects.

In my practice it has allowed me to help a pet achieve comfort without the use of harsh medications such as the non-steroidal anti-inflammatories or narcotics. If you combine acupuncture with oral herbal anti-inflammatories or herbal analgesics and topical essential oil massages, you will have a perfect recipe for quality and longevity of life!

Diet and other Natural Modalities

There is a lot to cover during a visit with an integrative doctor. I devoted an entire chapter in this book to species appropriate nutrition. It is vitally important that your pet's doctor speak with you about natural nutrition. My new client visits were commonly approaching three hours when I decided to create an informative DVD to save visit time. I now include this with all my new client consultations. In this DVD I educate my viewer about diet, vaccines, and titer testing, and other natural modalities such as essential oil usage and whole food supplementation.

I encourage a pet parent or veterinarian who is new to the usage of natural pet care to incorporate some of the easy to integrate modalities first. It is easy to decrease a vaccination protocol and it is easy to find good, free information on incorporating whole foods, super foods, and essential oils. Other modalities, such as acupuncture or veterinary spinal manipulative therapy require more extensive education and investment in time and money.

You should research the modalities that appeal to you and inquire whether your holistic veterinarian has a special focus for those or not. Inquiring clients continue to confuse the terminology holistic and homeopathic. It is important that you, the client and veterinary staff understand this terminology so that there is no confusion for you when scheduling an appointment.

Holistic Umbrella

Holistic is an umbrella term. If you are going to "Live with Your Pet in Mind", you should choose from modalities under this holistic umbrella for your pet care and your self-care.

Remember, a surgeon can practice holistically if he takes into consideration the entire mind, body and spirit of his patient. A good surgeon will discuss nutrition and lifestyle changes after he repairs a broken bone. An allopathic surgeon simply repairs the fracture and then moves on to his next patient.

Similarly, an acupuncturist may treat a group of patients like an assembly line with needles in and needles out. A good holistic acupuncturist will address nutrition, complementary herbal care and environmental factors contributing to the patient's imbalance.

VSMT

Under the umbrella, VSMT refers to Veterinary Spinal Manipulative Therapy. This is the term for veterinarians who pursue additional training to learn how to do adjustments on pets. Only human chiropractors who take additional training for practicing on animals can call themselves Animal Chiropractors. They are allowed to work on animals by referral from a veterinarian.

Herbs

Holistic veterinarians can focus on the utilization of Western and/or Chinese herbals in their practice if they participate in additional studies to learn how these plant formulations are used. There are many books, websites, and product literature to get you and your vet started on the road to incorporating these modalities into your pet's care.

Homeopathy

One of the many modalities under this holistic umbrella is homeopathy. Homeopathy used to be the primary form of medical care in this country until the allopathic medical establishment shut down the homeopathy schools. It is still a primary form of medicine in countries like Germany. Many quality homeopathic remedies are sourced from Europe.

You may have seen a popular homeopathic at health store check outs called Oscillococcinum®. This is a flu remedy. Surely you have seen the Zicam® commercials for colds. This too is a homeopathic. What is in these remedies? Essentially, nothing. Homeopathy is an energy medicine, which is quite difficult for most Western minds to comprehend, but that does not make it any less effective!

I practice very little homeopathy, although I have studied it and am familiar with some of the common remedies and have used some myself and on my patients. I have used the injectable Heel® products in some of my aquapuncture protocols.

I could not possibly do justice to homeopathy with a quick explanation here. However, my point is that if a client inquires as to whether Dr. Jodie practices homeopathy, sometimes they know what they are asking, and sometimes they do not. Sometimes they want a homeopathic remedy, but most of the time they are requesting general holistic care. Some individuals are not supportive of homeopathy and will lump all holistic practice into that misinformed impression.

Be sure to get clear for your pet's sake and yours, what type of holistic practice you are looking for. All holistic practitioners are not the same.

All holistic vets were originally, conventionally trained. We all know how to administer anesthesia, analgesics, anti-inflammatories and more. Holistic vets try hard to avoid drugs due to their side effects, but we all believe there is a time and place for them. I always explain this to my clients because I believe as part of informed consent laws, they should be told all their options, including benefits and risks of each.

Don't ever be afraid to respectfully question your vet's knowledge. You need to be your pet's advocate. There is a lot of information out there to learn and none of us can know everything. It is dangerous today to not educate yourself and it could harm your pet if you do not speak up!

Sitting on the Floor

Begin and End with a Cookie

In my opinion, to make a good visit a great one your holistic vet will spend most of his or her time on the floor with your pet and begin and end each session with a cookie!

I have been told that I am different from most vets because I spend a lot of time petting and explaining. Today's pet parent generally does not want to be told what to do. Would you agree that you prefer to be given all the information clearly, so that you can make your own informed decisions?

I enjoy having this chat while I sit on the floor with your pet, and gradually establish a rapport. Your pet will sense if we are having a good conversation and will also gravitate toward me as I will offer a meat-based treat or have one hidden under my leg.

Sometimes we will do a little "self-selection" with essential oils. I will set the bottles around the room. It is fun to see which ones resonate with your pet. Some clients bring a pendulum and dowse to select their products. Others use muscle testing. I stay open minded because I have learned a lot from my clients and from my patients! This all makes for great fun and it's nice when everyone is at ease!

CHAPTER 7

A Cozy Bed! *Natural Home Health*

All your pet wants after a full belly is a cozy bed in the sun, or a lap to snuggle in. Problem is, many times, our lap is occupied by a lap-top! All our living space is cluttered with technology emitting electromagnetic waves and bromide ions. You may not even be aware of the harm this exposure can cause to your dog or cat and they are unfortunately innocent bystanders in the toxic world that we have created!

It can be overwhelming to try to control the environment in which your pet lives, but there are some basic things you can do to replace toxins used in your home and on your pet and even on yourself! Start with knowledge, new habits, and essential oils!

Get Organized for Happiness

Begin with clear, organized thinking. This can help you focus and clean up your home environment. Conversely it is difficult to think clearly when sitting in a cluttered mess! Remember, how we think affects our emotions and physical health, so don't take this lightly! Clear the clutter! Productivity makes most people happier.

Household Toxins and Natural Cleaning

Now, when you begin cleaning, contrary to the popular commercial, you do not need bleach or other toxic antiseptics. The FDA just proclaimed a ban on many antibacterials. Triclosan a common antibacterial which was banned in Europe, but still utilized in many U.S. products had been shown to contribute to the rise of MRSA (methicillin resistant staph aureus) in hospitals.[1]

You can literally replace all the toxic cleaning products in your home with healthy essential oil blends. Let's start with the top of your head and the products that you use on your pet's fur.

Soaps

Shampoos are notorious for containing harsh, toxic even carcinogenic ingredients. Many also contain antimicrobial ingredients which destroy the natural microbiome on your scalp as well as your pet's skin. Remember, your hair and your skin is part of your pet's environment.

My dog loves to wrap himself in my hair. Dogs and sometimes kitties love to lick human skin. Sodium lauryl sulfate (SLS) is a soap ingredient which has been shown to denature protein and mimics estrogen. It can be a severe irritant. It may be contaminated with dioxane, a carcinogen, during processing.[2]

Many household products do not need to divulge all their ingredients for proprietary reasons, so it can be difficult to find safe products. SLS is often used in toothpastes. How would you like to find out that your pet got oral cancer from giving you kisses?

I do not know what I would do without **Revii Moisturizing Mineral Soap** in my practice. It is a human product but is great for pets because it is very mild and does not need to be rinsed off. It is perfect for mixing with essential oils. A healthy soap is often needed to emulsify and disperse essential oils when they are mixed in water. So, a small amount of this soap can be added to a water spritzer or into the bathtub. It is coconut oil based.
Who would have thought that you could share soap with your pet?

Conventional veterinarians and even many holistic veterinarians are hesitant to recommend essential oils for pets, however when grown, harvested, selected, prepared, and utilized properly, they can be an effective and safe modality to support a healthy human, dog or cat body!

Spot-ons

Sadly, many pet guardians are led to believe that it is necessary to apply a monthly spot-on pesticide to their pet's coat to prevent fleas and ticks from biting the pet.

Some of these products contain known carcinogens (permethrins) and others are suspected. Some cause itching and hair loss. During application, you are advised to wear gloves!

It is also interesting to note that most spot-ons do not deter the insect from biting the pet. The insect is killed after it bites the pet, and commonly after it transmits a disease it is carrying.

According to the National Pesticide Information Center, *"permethrin was classified by the International Agency for Research on Cancer (IARC) as "not classifiable as to its carcinogenicity to humans" in 1991. This means that IARC could not decide whether or not permethrin can cause cancer. The U.S. EPA decided that permethrin was "likely to be carcinogenic to humans" if it was eaten. This decision was based on the structure of permethrin, what happens to it in the body, laboratory tests that caused tumors in mice and evidence of tumors in rats."*[3]

Do you want to put this on the skin of an animal who licks himself daily? Most spot-ons are repeated monthly for the lifetime of the pet. I certainly am concerned about cumulative adverse effects.

Alternative Option & Essential Oils Safety[4, 5]

People put carcinogens, hormone disruptors and irritants in the midst of their family and pets every day, yet when you mention essential oils, the natural life blood of plants that are all around us, everyone gets in a tizzy about safety!

Oils are potent, but they are so beneficial, we should not be afraid to use them!

I do not recommend the repetitive use of "hot" oils, such as lemon grass, as spot-ons. Repetitive use in one location can cause the skin to scurf.

Essential oils such as cedar wood, lemongrass, peppermint, eucalyptus and citronella can provide an effective and healthy coat spray. However, poorly distilled, adulterated or improperly applied oils can also cause some serious problems!

I formulate a proprietary blend of the above oils called Furfume™ and Furfume Fire™. Each is mixed in distilled water with a few drops of healthy soap and then applied via a mister. I do not include citronella when I make my cat blend (Furfume™). I have had great feedback on both blends. Never saturate a coat. But, you do need to apply an all over shield.

Do not let cats ingest a significant amount of these oils. A light mist onto a towel and the rubbed over your cat is adequate. Even the ingestion of outdoor plants can cause vomiting, diarrhea and dehydration when too much is ingested. **Always remember if an essential oil gets on a mucous membrane or in an eye, dilute the adverse effect with vegetable oil, not water!**

Tea Tree, Melaleuca or Melrose™ Blend

Tea tree or melaleuca has a reputation for causing illness in some dogs and cats. Yet blends of therapeutic grade oils containing melaleuca have been used successfully on many pets when applied in small amounts or when diluted properly with a healthy vegetable oil such as olive or coconut oil. These fatty oils (vegetable oils) are called carrier oils. These fatty oils can be used to dilute essential oils. But, beware, carrier oils taste delicious and encourage the pet to lick and ingest.

Thieves®

We use a blend of clove, lemon, cinnamon bark, eucalyptus, and rosemary to clean our stainless steel exam tables, our windows, to mop our floors and even to shine our mirrors! You can too.

Microbes are becoming increasingly resistant to conventional antibiotics, and topical disinfectants can adversely affect the immune systems and organs of humans and pets who encounter them. Essential oils offer a healthy alternative for this dilemma.

In my practice, this same blend has saved dogs from toe amputation due to antibiotic-resistant nail bed infections.

The most important location for its use is in our Kitty Kamp, our non-profit residence for our iPAW kitties. We have diffused and cleaned without adversity for more than a decade.

This same blend can be put with safe, natural soaps for use in your laundry and can be applied to dryer balls. Keep toxic detergent and dryer sheet residues off your clothing and bedding which touches your pet's fur.

Toxic Sprays and Perfumes

Living with your pet in mind, means putting your pet's health (and your own) above your glamour.
Think about the hairspray and the perfume that is aerosolized and falls over your pet's head. The first thing your pet does when you pick him up is lick your neck.

Toxins in perfumes, due to chemical solvent extraction and laboratory synthesized fragrances, and in hair sprays are well-documented. Sadly, when some guardians walk into the clinic with a pet with cancer, I can tell by the smell of perfume, hair spray or smoke why their pet might have developed cancer, asthma, or skin disease. We will discuss this further in Chapter 8 on Self-Care.

Lawn Care

Pet and human cancer has been correlated with herbicides and pesticides used outdoors. Dogs roll and lie in the grass. Dogs and cats eat grass. Lawn care chemicals have residuals. This is why they prevent weeds from growing over a long period of time.

So, don't believe for a second that your lawn is safe "when the chemicals are dry"! That is not even a funny joke. There are companies that utilize tea compost, worms, corn-based treatments and aeration to control weeds.

So, please don't stress or worry over this discussion. View this as a new awareness or an opportunity to recommit. Be concerned and take action! If you are stressed, this next suggestion is for you!

Lavender

Perhaps, the oil with the most notoriety and diversity of uses is lavender. Lavender is emotionally calming, topically soothing, supports healthy skin and is orally delicious when used to make ice cream!

An internationally acclaimed organic farm which harvests and distills its own lavender provides visitors with therapeutic grade lavender products which can be consumed internally. I have used lavender to soothe my own burns, insect, and cat bite wounds. It can be applied with Vitamin E to incisions and supports healthy skin of dogs and cats.

Home Diffusing for Pets

When you choose an essential oil for your pet, be sure that it can be used internally, even if your intent is to only use it externally. This speaks to the quality of the oil, the safety, and its efficacy. If a human can ingest it, then it will be OK if your pet licks it.

However, be cautious with "hot oils", which may contain phenols, which felines cannot metabolize properly because they lack some of the normal human and dog-- liver detoxification enzymes. Cinnamon, oregano, thyme, and clove are examples. One drop of oil goes a long way for a kitty just as for a human infant.

Quality oils can be expensive, but small amounts can be quite effective. Always be sure the pet can get away from the diffused oils. Never confine them in a closed room with a diffuser.

Exposing a cat who has severely congested nasal passages to a blend of ravensara, eucalyptus, peppermint, wintergreen and lemon in a cold air diffuser which nebulizes the oils can be more than comforting! For cats who are difficult to medicate, this approach can be a life saver! I am speaking from personal experience in my veterinary practice.

Peace and Calming I or II, Valor I or II, Stress Away, T-Away

Think of these blends for relaxation or bravery. These blends contain some single oils that create peace and calm just thinking about them: vanilla, tangerine, blue tansy.

Treating pet behavioral disorders with antipsychotic meds is in vogue. Veterinarians do not yet know what long term side effects may occur from these drugs. We are fortunate to have the option to massage our pets using calming essential oils or to simply utilize aromatherapy. There are clip on collar diffusers available and auto diffusers so that pets can be exposed to these oils easily and in a variety of environments.

Alternative modalities can be integrated into conventional pet care. Essential oils are a great example of how natural subtances can be safe and effective. To get started with your new resolution, contact a holistic veterinarian who is experienced with using oils on dogs and cats.

Is Someone's Bad Habit Making Your Pet Sick?

I am baffled by how many people still smoke. I continue to have pet-loving guardians tell me, "but, I smoke outside, or my spouse smokes outside." This statement continues to show how naïve people are in regard to the effects on others of second hand smoke.

When I review a radiograph of a pet who has a primary lung tumor my heart sinks. This is a needless loss of a beautiful life.

What does your dog do the minute you enter the home? Sniffs you up and down, right? We all know how sensitive their noses are! And of course there are the little ones who curl up in your lap and lie right on the residue. Then, they groom themselves and eat it. Those of us who do not smoke can smell the lingering residue on a smoker's clothes or even in their hair! Don't forget about the household teenager who thinks they are being sneaky and hiding their habit yet exposing their own beloved pet!

A case-control study of nasal cancer in pet dogs was conducted to test the hypothesis that exposure to environmental tobacco smoke increases risk. The data support an association between environmental tobacco smoke and canine nasal cancer.[6]

Passive smoking may increase the risk of malignant lymphoma in cats and (that) further study of this relation in humans is warranted.[7] Some inhabitants of homes with smokers have suggested air purifiers to be a solution. I would suggest take great caution with the placement of the air purifier in your home.
It is common to place the equipment in a location which actually drags the toxins through the air, across the path of the pet or even near the areas where the pet or family frequent. This actually concentrates the exposure risk. Don't forget, residues even fall into the pet's water bowl!

While a smoker is kicking the habit, clothing should be stripped, and hair washed upon entering the home. Your pet should not be allowed into the same car where a smoker has been.

If your pet has asthma, sinusitis, a difficult to manage skin condition or anything which is being called an allergy, regard this as a potential pre-cancerous condition and question this pet's exposure to potential toxins such as second or third hand smoke.

So, let's say you have decided to give it up and clean the air! Reach for your oils once again!

Purification™

There is an excellent oil blend which freshens the air and eliminates odors. It is a combination of citronella, lemongrass, lavandin, rosemary, tea tree, and myrtle. This can be used in your home in an ultrasonic or nebulizing diffuser. We use this blend almost daily in my veterinary practice. We diffuse it in our Kitty Kamp, our non-profit area where several unadoptable cats live.

We also mist it on the butts of dogs after they have had their anal glands expressed!

I put it on my arm after I got a spider bite in my barn.

This blend contains natural chemical constituents: cineol, neral, and geranial. It is fun and helpful to google these constituents. See what research has shown them to be able to do!

I suggest that you google the particular oil constituents whenever you would like to understand better how an oil works and to best utilize it for yourself, your family and for your pet!

CHAPTER 8

Loving Guardian   *Pet Parent(s) Self-care*

Your cat cares about your good health, although she would never admit it. Your dog thrives on your good health. Your dog is likely devastated when you are not well. How you feel affects how you think and what you say. It can be difficult to care for another when you are not well yourself.

Pet Parent Coaching

To be a truly holistic veterinarian, I have come to believe that I must coach pet guardians to fully help their pets. During a typical visit we always spend a lot of time talking about natural pet nutrition, and invariably the pet parent comments, "This dog (or this cat) is going to be eating better than me." It is sad to think that may be true!

Overweight, sedentary pet guardians often have overweight pets. Anxious pet parents often share space with neurotic pets. Owner and pet habits and disorders often mirror each other.

I am quite adamant about species appropriate diet for carnivores as the best path to great health. But does this philosophy pertain to human dietary choices? For myself, I have chosen to eat a vegetarian diet. I have had that focus for most of my life. I have adhered to this the best I could since about seventh grade. I was vegan for a couple years. I found that to be quite difficult. I continue to practice this way for primarily moral reasons. I cannot treat animals all day and then eat them at night!

In my heart, I do believe that we are primates, and other than consuming some insects, I am pretty sure gorillas are vegetarians. That being said, I respect what I was taught by the Institute for Integrative Nutrition® about **bioindividuality**. People are different. We all come from many different cultural and familial back grounds. One type of diet may work very well for one individual, but not so well for another.

I am not going to judge how people choose to eat. But, if they are complaining about their situation or if they ask my guidance, I have been trained to coach them to do better with their food choices. I can recognize how some of their mental choices and physical practices may be adversely impacting their pet.

Eat Fresh Food

During my nutrition program, we learned a little about hundreds of diets. It was interesting how the proponents of each were so convincing about the benefits of their particular program. What I found most impactful is what our main instructor, Joshua Rosenthal emphasized. All good diets have one guiding principle in common. Eat fresh food!

This mandate is important for our pets and for us. We also talked, earlier in Chapter 5, about how important it is that you learn to read the ingredient labels on pet foods and treats, same goes for your foods! Ideally, if you shop the perimeter of the store, there will be very few labels! Your food labels can be mis-leading, just like your pet's food labels. Remember to always look at the back. Never rely on the deception of the front label. I think the greatest disservice to the American public in this regard has been the terminology lite and lo-fat.

Lo-fat Myth

The American consumer has been led to believe that foods which are lite, or lo-fat are better for you and better for weight management. Unfortunately, lo-fat commonly means high sugar. Lite commonly means low calorie which may mean no sugar, but instead artificial sweeteners or poor-quality fats.

Avoid foods with those labels. Buy fresh or look for real foods on ingredient panels.

The second most common mistake is not noticing the number of calories per serving and not realizing how many servings are in the package. This is another common reason for over consumption of calories. Many people glance at the label and assume the number of calories listed is for the entire package. This is not so.

So, how do you feel you are doing in the grocery store?

Exercise

Is shopping your only form of exercise? Who needs a FitBit when you have dogs? My five rescues keep me busy! Currently, I have three little dogs and two cats. They range in age from eight to eighteen. Each has an issue that needs frequent attention.

It is great how you can combine pet care with self-care! Sometimes, those little darlin's force you to take care of yourself!

I am sharing space with three little pee'ers. I used to hate that word, pee. Had to use the veterinary lingo, urinate. Pee is urine. To pee is to urinate. Somehow, the quick whiz on every furniture corner, bush, fire hydrant and telephone pole does seem more appropriately dubbed pee. I have come to accept this terminology because I must describe this substance and act, so frequently. My three keep me remarkably busy. I love to sit in my chair and do Facebook, respond to emails, and write this book. It is said that you should get up every 15 minutes so that your body doesn't cramp up. No worries here!

Some dog is always whining to go outside or waking up out of a drunken stupor and stumbling towards a furniture corner to lift a leg, and I do not mean the chair leg! So, let me tell you, I really need to put a positive twist on this neediness to believe it helps me with my self-care! Yep, it's great exercise, right? Up and down.

Pet Selection for Happiness

Quality pet care and good self-care begins with pet selection. A bad match, like a bad marriage can lead to life-long stress. Put some time and thought into your pet adoption or purchase!

It's great when a Border collie chooses an athletic guardian. How I admire the fit guardian of an agility athlete! My favorite part of watching an agility trial is watching those dogs do those weave poles. What great exercise and emotional fitness for the owners and those talented pets!

Athletic pets (sled dogs, search and rescue dogs, canine officers) have such amazing bonds with their guardians.

Whether you are in that athletic category or not, all pets want you to participate in their lives! They want you to be well so that you can respond to their needs and to their love.

What about those sad eyes staring at you when you are too busy to go for a walk and then that excited spin when you put on your shoes and grab the leash? What does it mean when a frustrated cat begins to spray all over your house? What does it mean when your kitty drops a dead mouse at your door? Good or bad, they are interacting with you.

These are all behaviors and gestures with specific meaning between you and your pet. I hope that you recognize the important place you hold in the mind of your pet.

If you want to be alive and well for a long time for the sake of your pet, then let us consider some self-care. I have noticed many pet guardians spend a lot of time worrying about their pet but take extremely poor care of themselves. If you are among those guardians who would say, "This guy is going to be eating better than me"; let us change that!

Identify, Avoid, or Replace

Where do we start? Recognition! Recognize what is wrong with our nutrition, self-care choices or lifestyle and then change. Identify, avoid, or replace. The average American diet is horrific. This is why it has been called SAD, the Standard American Diet! Let's start with that sad realization.
We talked about the excesses and deficiencies in our pets' processed foods, are our options any better? Let us talk about the United States toxic, processed food supply and even unhealthy supplements! We need to learn to identify, avoid and replace. Look at this list. Can you identify how many of these items you consume?

The Top Toxic Substances
Eaten Daily by Americans[1]

☐ Diet soda, sports drinks, sweetened beverages
☐ Bakery, breads, pasta
☐ Processed foods
☐ Canned foods
☐ Non-organic fruits, vegetables, dairy, meat
☐ Cooked or charred meat (heterocyclic amines)
☐ Coffee
☐ Synthetic vitamins and minerals
☐ Toxic packaging

You notice I have not included alcohol, cigarettes, or other drugs. To me, these are no brainers. By that I mean people consuming them *inappropriately* have no brain. Harsh? I have had to console pet guardians whose pet had developed lung cancer due to second or third hand smoke! (See Chapter 7) It is difficult to have sympathy when the individual knows better.

I realize how difficult an addiction can be, but there is no excuse for putting an innocent loved one at risk. Also, there has been a lot of public education on alcohol, cigarettes, and drugs. The adversity is obvious. Do you think your pet wants to be in the car with you when you are driving drunk? Your little buddy needs you home to make dinner, not out being reckless due to alcohol abuse or drug use.

I am still caring for a patient who I helped to re-home. This little dog's former guardian brought him in for severe allergies, but, we have reason to suspect the spouse was involved with a meth lab in the home. The entire family was ill. People in these situations need to wake up! Self-care is not just for yourself when you have a family or a pet.

Many of the foods in the previous list are not as obvious, so examining these are more important, so that you might develop awareness as to why they are so detrimental to your health. I feel sorry for the unknowing public who is duped by the industries that make our foods and the commercial industry that misleads us every day!

Let's see if I can convince you why you should avoid these top toxic substances and then suggest how you can replace them with healthier options.

✓ Diet soda, sports drinks, sweetened beverages

Step 1: Identify, Avoid, and Replace Toxic or Sugary Drinks

Soda, sport drinks, and yes, even those cold teas may contain **artificial sweeteners** such as saccharin, and aspartame (NutraSweet, Equal).[2] These substances can alter brain neurochemistry! Some drinks still contain **high fructose corn syrup,** which is now hidden by using other names. And, even if natural cane sugar is used, this is still a major source of excessive carbohydrate consumption in this country.[3]

Avoid all of these and drink water instead! You or the manufacturer can replace artificial sweeteners with stevia in your drinks. I just saw the new Coke in a green colored bottle which contains some stevia and cane sugar. I would still never drink it, but I suppose it is an improvement.

Usually when your body craves something to drink, it is craving water. Your mind might be craving sugar or alcohol. When you try to satisfy your craving with soda or a stiff drink, you perpetuate your problem.

Many flavored drinks contain substances which make you hungry. They may even work on the nervous system to stimulate your appetite. So, recognize this and for three weeks, use will power and replacement to satiate your cells with fresh water!

Aspartame has side effects. Even shortly after it was first approved, which only took one year, the FDA had recorded 600 consumer complaints of headaches, dizziness, and other health-related reactions from its consumption.
Other problems linked to aspartame consumption have included weight gain, vision problems, depression, and mood changes, and even brain cancer. [4]

In 1992, the United States Air Force issued a warning to pilots to avoid products containing aspartame (NutraSweet/Equal and others) because it has been linked to seizures, vertigo, dizziness, sudden memory loss, and gradual loss of vision.

Seizures are a primary side effect of aspartame consumption. As if that were not disturbing enough, they occur in people who've never had a seizure before and disappear just as quickly when aspartame consumption is stopped.

MIT conducted a survey of 80 seizure sufferers. Survey results showed the role aspartame played in those seizures met FDA criteria for an imminent hazard to the public's health. This measure is what the FDA *normally* relies upon to pull unsafe products from the market.

To further dupe the unknowing consumer, the manufacturers of aspartame are now changing the name of this substance to Amino Sweet.[5]

Splenda or sucralose has been linked to cancer in mice and rats.[6] I never use those little packets available in a restaurant or hotel. Ask for them to provide you with honey for your coffee or tea! Consumer pressure creates change!

Natural Sweeteners

High Fructose Corn Syrup, Sugar

You know excess sugar is detrimental; high fructose corn syrup (HFCS) is a hidden sugar!

Fructose is a sweetener usually derived from corn, and is now the single largest calorie source of Americans. Fifty-five percent of sweeteners used by food and beverage manufacturers today are made from HFCS, because it's cheaper and 20 percent sweeter than regular table sugar (sucrose).

The number one source of calories in the United States today is soda, which is primarily sweetened with HFCS. The over consumption of sugar or High Fructose Corn Syrup (HFCS) is the major factor in increasing rates of obesity and chronic diseases all over the world.[7]

The average American consumes 47 pounds of cane sugar and 35 pounds of high fructose corn syrup every year! Is that you?

I always try to emphasize to my clients that sugar causes inflammation. It can be difficult to understand that mechanism, but sometimes until we understand, we cannot believe. The sugar to inflammation connection is in something science calls advanced glycation end products (ages). Sugars are pro-inflammatory agents that create these advanced glycation end products (AGEs). They speed up the aging process![8]

Excessive sugar consumption leads to **insulin resistance** and growth of fat cells around your vital organs! This scenario is a risk factor for chronic disease. [9]

Sugar or High Fructose Corn Syrup (HFCS) excess is linked to:

* Insulin resistance and obesity
* Elevated blood pressure
* Elevated triglycerides and LDL (bad) cholesterol
* Depletion of vitamins and minerals
* Cardiovascular disease, liver disease, cancer, arthritis, and gout

Sarahbel's Story

Do you know anyone with any of these issues? I hope it is not you! Remember, your pet hopes it is not you either, and I hope it is not your pet! Schnauzers are predisposed to high triglycerides. This often causes them to develop pancreatitis. When I help convert them to a meat-based diet and get them off the carbs, their triglycerides normalize!

I care for a sweet little Schnauzer named Sarahbel. Her parents are senior snow birders. They are very dedicated to Sarahbel's health and their own. When they learned about all the starch in dry kibble as a source of sugar for Sarahbel and they saw the decrease in her triglyceride levels when we changed her over to the raw diet, they were ecstatic! They researched where they could get good quality foods in Florida for Sarahbel and for themselves!

Is agave good?

Remember, the danger of sugar is a dosing issue – small doses (of sugars) are harmless, large doses over time will kill you! Agave is a "natural" sweetener. However, most agave is WORSE than HFCS because it has higher fructose content than any commercial sweetener -- ranging from 70 to 97 percent, depending on the brand, which is FAR HIGHER than HFCS, which averages 55 percent! Blue Agave may be better.[10]

Fructose is metabolized to fat in your body far more rapidly than any other sugar. The burden of metabolizing fructose falls on your liver, and it promotes a particularly dangerous kind of body fat or adipose tissue! This is the type of fat that collects in your abdominal region and is associated with a greater risk of heart disease!

Is stevia the hero?

Stevia has been used in Paraguay for centuries and in Japan for decades. It is not a "new" sweetener.[11] There has been an FDA battle over allowing it as a food additive vs. dietary supplement.

The plain leaves are pleasantly sweet and NOT metallic. Separating it into its chemical constituents allows for patenting, but this changes the flavor. This is why so many people feel that Stevia is bitter and don't like it.

Dr. Joe Mercola says, "*Personally I believe stevia is the best sweetener available today and is the one I personally use and travel with. Some people object to a bitter metallic type of aftertaste but it has been my experience this is related to the way the stevia plant is processed. If you were to eat the whole fresh leaf of the plant, there is no metallic aftertaste.*"

So, if you are one who has objected to the taste of stevia, consider using a different brand until you find one that tastes good! You can purchase some good ones here:
www.mercola.com
www.longevitywarehouse.com
I have purchased mine from David Wolfe at Longevity Warehouse. I love the vanilla version!

Is Truvia a brand of stevia? [12]

No! Cargill and Coca-Cola manufacture Truvia. PureVia, a competitor to Truvia created by PepsiCo, also extracts an ingredient from the stevia leaf called "Reb A." through a proprietary technology using ethanol. Truvia also contains erythritol (a sugar alcohol like xylitol) and "natural flavors." Sugar alcohols like erythritol and xylitol, while being somewhat better than artificial sweeteners, are not truly "natural" sweeteners. The final word on sugar alcohols as a group seems to be a mixed message. The evidence does seem to support the positive claims made on behalf of these sweeteners, but one single factor from a natural food item is being isolated from its normal co-constituents and consumed at levels that are difficult to obtain when eating the food item itself.

Nutrition Conspiracies

Why aren't Coke and other companies using just plain stevia to sweeten their beverages? Monsanto spent 20 years blocking the FDA's approval of stevia when they thought it posed a threat to NutriSweet. The FDA approved Truvia in three weeks, even giving it the coveted GRAS (generally regarded as safe) status.[13]

Brominated vegetable oil (BVO) keeps the flavor oils contained in soda in suspension. BVO is like an emulsifier, helping to disperse the flavor oils throughout the product.[14]

What is commercial soda anyway?

Why spend so much time being concerned about it? We should be sure that anything we put a lot of into our bodies is healthy. And, surely, Americans put a lot of soda into their bodies! This beverage is generally made of chemicals or sugar and chemicals. Sugar and bromine and aluminum and BPA and HFCS and dye...
What is bromine/bromide? It is a halide. Remember chemistry class?

Alert: halides: bromide, fluoride, chloride can replace iodide in your body (or your pet's)

Iodine deficiency can lead to hypothyroidism and cancer!
Do you know anyone with that? I hope it is not you! It is me. I have hypothyroidism. I drank Cherry Coke and ate M&M's to get me through many a long night studying for exams in veterinary school. Let us learn more about this bromide/iodine relationship and how it can affect us and our pets.[15]

More on Brominated vegetable oil (BVO)

In April 2015, Coca-Cola and PepsiCo agreed to remove brominated vegetable oil (BVO) from all their beverages in the *near* future. First patented as a flame retardant, BVO contains bromine. Bromine accumulates in bodies and breast milk. It is a toxic endocrine disruptor.

146

Remember biology? Your endocrine glands include things like the thyroid gland, pancreas, thymus, ovaries, testicles, etc. So, this BVO damages your thyroid and leads to cancer, infertility, schizophrenia, and more.

BVO is banned in Europe and Japan, but in the US it is still permitted under "interim" status, pending safety studies—for the last 44 years! The FDA says studying BVO is not a priority. BVO shares interim status with saccharin. Saccharin has been on and off and back on the market several times.[16]

What else is brominated? Bread is also brominated. This makes it white. If you don't know it already, in nutrition, white is bad! (White sugar, white flour, and white pasta!)

Let's identify a couple more categories of unhealthy beverages and then talk about how to replace them!

Energy Drinks

When consumed over a long term, one study confirmed that, in college-age men, energy drinks can cause anxiety, dehydration, insomnia, and cardiovascular vascular problems. A separate study, by the American Heart Association, found that consuming just one sixteen-ounce energy drink elevates blood pressure and stress-hormone responses in young, healthy adults.

Does your husband, so or brother drink a lot of these? How have they been sleeping? Any one you know have restless leg syndrome? Stop with the energy drinks and no carbs before bed! [17]

Fruit Juice

Really? I'm going to pick on fruit juice? Yes! I have an overweight friend who drinks a lot of fruit juice and even when she tries to do a detox, she continues to put a lot of fruit in her shakes. She has trouble with the awareness of the incredible amount of sugar in concentrated fruit juice. In addition to fruit juice being another source of a lot of sugar in our diet, it is a big source of pesticides.[18]

Certainly, there is a nutritional benefit of vitamins and other nutrients in fruit juices vs. other synthetic beverages. But the number of pesticides and the concentration of sugar should not be overlooked. Orange juice and strawberries are the most pesticide-laden crops. Choose your fruits by using the glycemic index. The lower a food's glycemic index or glycemic load, the less it affects blood sugar and insulin levels.[3]

Of course, we can replace all unhealthy beverages with fresh, clean water! That is a whole other complicated topic, isn't it?! Many have lost weight simply by replacing soda with water.

For those who are addicted physically or out of habit to soda, high sugar juices or teas or energy drinks, it can be helpful to choose alternative beverages as steppingstones to only water. These alternatives can also be helpful in social situations. These can provide you or a teen with the "I'm drinking something cool" factor.

Young Living has developed some great replacement drinks. Zyng is their carbonated beverage and healthy answer to soda. They use sparkling water, pear and blackberry juices, and a hint of lime and black pepper essential oils.

Ningxia Nitro is their answer to high energy products like Red Bull. The ingredients in this product are amazing! It is delicious and can be stored in your purse or jean pocket. [19, 20]

Ningxia Nitro Ingredients
D-ribose
Green tea extract
Mulberry leaf extract
Korean ginseng extract
Choline
Vanilla oil
Chocolate oil
Yerba mate oil
Spearmint, peppermint, nutmeg, black pepper oils
Wolfberry seed oil
Berry juice blend, coconut nectar
Natural flavor, pectin, xanthan gum
B-vitamins, iodine
D-ribose

D-ribose is a simple sugar found naturally in the body. The production of D-ribose is initiated by cultivating B. subtilis (a "good" bacterium, followed by fermentation, during which glucose is converted to D-ribose.
The backbone for RNA and DNA, D-ribose is also involved in the creation of ATP (cellular energy). It is used in the health field to increase muscle energy and improve exercise performance. In a study, D-ribose significantly reduced clinical symptoms in patients suffering from fibromyalgia and chronic fatigue syndrome. [21]

Juice your own organic veggies!

This is probably the most important thing you could do for self-care! Other than positive mind set, I believe juicing organic veggies daily is the thing that makes me feel best daily. I thought this would be difficult and avoided doing this thinking I would not have time to set up and clean the juicer. Thankfully, my daughter gave me a juicer one year for Mother's Day. It was easy and the output was delicious! I make a point to always rinse it immediately and I have been incredibly happy with bringing this good habit into my life! Juicers are cheap. A great tip is to pour your freshly blended juice over ice. You can do this! And guess what? You can give some of your veggie juice to your pet!

What other sweeteners should you be aware of?

Xylitol is a commonly used sweetener which seems to be okay for most humans but is highly toxic to pets. It is not used in drinks but many other things you might eat, store in your purse, leave on your countertop, where your pet might have access.

My main caution here is to be sure that your pet does not get into any of your products which contain this substance. Xylitol is used in gum and even health supplements. It is also used to flavor human medications.

When non-primate species (dogs) eat something containing xylitol, the xylitol is quickly absorbed into the bloodstream, resulting in a potent release of insulin from the pancreas.

This causes profound hypoglycemia (low blood sugar) and is life threatening. Be aware of this if "sharing" human health supplements with your pet! Be aware of this if you choose to purchase pet medications through a human pharmacy![22]

Does xylitol cause any human side effects? Should you eat it? The body cannot digest xylitol properly. The non-metabolized portion ferments and creates a favorable environment for harmful bacteria to colonize, exacerbating yeast problems. Unmetabolized toxins sit in your fat, contributing to inability to clear fat, and then cause you to gain weight.

The key to the xylitol side effects is in its dosage. The main adverse effects reported from oral xylitol use at a dosage exceeding 40 to 50 g/day included nausea, bloating, diarrhea.

On the flip side, xylitol has oral health benefits in addition to sweetening. This is why it is intentionally used in gum and a lot of good quality toothpastes. This ingredient is used in the Young Living AromaBright toothpaste. I do use this toothpaste. I also use a charcoal/probiotic toothpaste. Often the key to nutritional safety and balance lies in moderation or in variety and rotation of foods or supplements, or self-care products in general.

✓ Bakery, breads, pasta

Step 2: Identify, Avoid, and Replace Toxic Bakery, Breads, Pasta
Identify foods with hidden or excess refined sugars, trans fats, or gliaden.

Refined Sugar
What is so bad about sugar? It is natural isn't it?
High consumption of sugar leads to elevated insulin levels.

Insulin puts excess sugar into storage, as triglycerides. Triglycerides are the fat storage form of carbohydrates. Excess sugar is a problem, but excess refined sugar is worse! The symptoms are weight gain, bloating, fatigue, arthritis, migraines, lowered immune function, gallstones, obesity, breast cancer, gum disease, cavities, and cardiovascular disease. Weston Price studies compared the beautiful teeth of children eating raw sugar cane to the decayed teeth of children eating refined sugar. The trouble is the chemicals used to refine! [23]

Sugar handling balance is a key factor in the role that sugar plays in good or poor health. Candy causes insulin release like a firework. Starch causes insulin release like a grand finale! Your bakery breads, pasta and your pet's kibble, are loaded with starch!

Avoid or replace refined sugar with raw cane sugar or stevia. Replace starchy bakery, breads or pasta with vegetable side dishes, with spaghetti squash or berry desserts.

Partially Hydrogenated Vegetable Oil

This is made by reacting vegetable oil with hydrogen. The level of polyunsaturated oils (good fat) is reduced and trans fats are created. **Trans fats** are present in some vegetable shortening, margarines, crackers, candies, baked goods, cookies, snack foods, fried foods, salad dressings, and many other processed foods. Trans fats are associated with heart disease, breast and colon cancer, atherosclerosis and elevated cholesterol. Could you even go to a fast-food facility and not consume fried foods? These should NEVER be consumed! Margarine was the demise of society. [24]

Eat butter! Try to obtain raw butter. Butter from pastured animals is the healthiest, most delicious, and best for the animals that provided it for you.

Use extra virgin olive oil in salad dressings or with vinaigrette. Use coconut oil or grapeseed oil for cooking. These measures will greatly reduce trans fats in your diet.

Gluten/Gliaden

Gluten is all the buzz, but is there really anything to be concerned about? And what is gliaden?
Many articles and books explain the negative impact that these substances have had on our society and why this is a relatively recent phenomenon. Gluten is a wheat protein. Technically, it is a large molecule made up of glutenin and gliadin. These proteins contain a particular peptide sequence which intolerant immune systems perceive as a foreign invader. Immune systems, such as that in people with Crohn's, celiac disease or other autoimmune disorders such as Hashimoto's autoimmune thyroiditis cannot handle these foreign invaders.

Read the Wheat Belly book by Dr. William Davis. It is a life changer! Concerns regarding gluten are not just a fad nor just a concern for those diagnosed with Crohn's disease. Wheat of today is not the same as our wheat of yesteryear. The number of chromosomes is actually different.

Wheat was modified. Its size was changed to withstand weather damage. This helped farmers avoid financial ruin, but inadvertently made the wheat higher in gluten. Levels are so high that they are intolerable for many consumers. Gluten's presence can put a person with Crohn's into writhing pain and exacerbate autoimmune disorders, such as the Hashimoto's autoimmune thyroiditis, which millions of people, like me, attempt to manage daily. [25]

Do you know if you have an autoimmune disorder? Many common disorders are now being linked to an autoimmune cause, even arthritis. The most common canine thyroid disease is also an autoimmune thyroiditis causing hypothyroidism. Research is needed as to cause an effect that diet plays on the expression of this disorder in dogs. However, common sense tells me to avoid wheat in carnivore canine diets and coach you to avoid processed wheat pasta and wheat bread!

The whole wheat trend has always been a farce. Whole wheat flour is no better than white, other than the lack of bleaching. It is a joke, like grain-free foods for dogs. Whole wheat flour is processed and full of starchy flour. It is not at all the same as what is meant by whole grain. A whole grain is slower to digest than flour. Therefore, there is a slower insulin release, which is a positive.

✓ Processed foods, canned foods

Step 3:
Identify, Avoid, and Replace Processed and Canned Foods

Processed foods are not fresh. They commonly contain artificial preservatives such as BHA or BHT, natural flavors such as MSG and maybe, nitrates or nitrites.

I can still remember years ago debating with the Hill's pet food rep over whether it was a good idea that their processed foods contained BHA, BHT and even ethoxyquin. It is hard to believe 15 years later, these have finally been removed from most of their foods, yet some are still present in children's' cereals! [26]

Studies have shown these artificial preservatives to be carcinogenic in rats. **Butylated hydroxyanisole (BHA)** is a potent antioxidant. Therefore, it is used as a preservative. It can help prevent mold. Funny that it is a food additive which the FDA deems "generally recognized as safe" (GRAS), yet the National Institutes of Health (NIH) says it is "reasonably anticipated to be a human carcinogen". Which is it? In any case, I am reading labels and avoiding BHA. It is found in potato chips, lard, butter, cereal, instant mashed potatoes, preserved meat, beer, baked goods, dry beverages, and dessert mixes, chewing gum, wax food packaging and more.[27]

Sodium nitrates and nitrites are contained in canned foods and processed foods such as bacon, sausage, corned beef, ham, hot dogs, and lunch meats. Nitrite inhibits rancid off-flavors, creates the characteristic pink color of cured meat, and inhibits the growth of food spoiling bacteria, such as Clostridium botulinum, which produces a deadly neurotoxin.

Nitrite, in high concentrations, is toxic to us. Accidental ingestion in contaminated drinking water, or too much mixed into sausages or medicines can cause methemoglobinemia. You may have heard of this as an often-fatal condition in newborns (blue baby syndrome). [28]

There is an unusually high incidence of esophageal cancer in Henan Province, China. This has been associated with a diet of vegetables pickled in water containing high levels of nitrate and nitrite.

Due to the risk of toxicity and cancer, the amount of nitrite added to foods is beginning to be restricted. You can find products labeled: No nitrates.

One solution is, do not eat processed lunch meats!

Natural flavors sound okay, don't they? The phrase natural flavors is commonly a way to "hide" MSG on your label. Monosodium Glutamate (MSG) is a flavor enhancer for processed foods. It is an excitotoxin. MSG adversely affects nerve cells in the brain. Many people get a headache, even a migraine when they consume MSG. [29]

MSG inhibits natural growth hormone, contributes to obesity, and in addition to causing headaches, it may cause nausea, weakness, a burning sensation in the back of neck and forearms, wheezing, and changes in heart rate.
Can you believe it is found in infant formula, low fat milk, candy, chewing gum, drinks, over-the-counter medications (especially children's), fruit yogurts, prescription drugs, intravenous fluids, and even the chicken pox vaccine?

To remove MSG from your diet, you will need to remove foods with the following ingredients on their label: monosodium glutamate, free glutamate hydrolyzed proteins (any type), autolyzed yeast, yeast extract caseinate, "natural" or artificial flavors.

Are there "natural flavors" that are okay? Maybe, but there is another scary natural flavor. It is diacetyl. This provides the "natural" butter flavor in microwave popcorn. Diacetyl causes bronchiolitis obliterans, commonly known as "popcorn lung". This is a debilitating disorder. This condition is afflicting the food chemists and other employees who are involved in the manufacture of this substance. Natural flavors are called such because they are derived from a natural substance, but the processing of them often creates a danger.

What is the solution? Avoid processed foods; eat fresh! Shop the perimeter of the grocery store!

Other Concerns for Self-Care

✓ Non-organic fruits, vegetables, dairy, meat

Step 4: Identify, Avoid, and Replace Antibiotics, Hormones, Pesticides, GMO foods and cruelly- produced products

Non-organic fresh foods may:
- Contain antibiotics
- Contain hormones
- Contain pesticides
- Be Genetically Modified Organisms (GMO)
- Be from animals who have been inhumanely treated

Antibiotics in your food, as medicine and antibacterials

Standard factory farming produces poor quality milk, cheese, eggs and produce. Crowding and subsequent stress causes poor growth and salmonella proliferation and shedding.

The farming solution has been to misuse antibiotics to maintain health and increase growth. Excessive antibiotic and antibacterial use in livestock production and household care has contributed to world-wide bacterial resistance. How does bacteria resistance impact us personally?

Dr. Oz did one of his great audience participation demonstrations to explain this concept of bacterial resistance. As usual, he chose a poor woman from the audience. Thankfully, this demo wasn't as embarrassing as some. Dr. Oz gave the woman a pin and told her that her pin was the antibiotic. On a large peg board were a multitude of balloons representing bacteria. The balloons were comprised of three different colors as follows:

White balloons =probiotics, "good" bacteria
Yellow balloons = infection, "bad" bacteria
Red balloons = resistant bacteria, "superbugs"

There were lots of white balloons. There were quite a few, but less yellow balloons. There were very few red balloons.
The woman was instructed to begin popping balloons, but because the red balloons were resistant to her antibiotic pin, she was told she could not pop any red balloons.
As she randomly popped the white and yellow balloons, the yellow infection quickly disappeared, but, as she continued the antibiotic pin popping, beyond resolution of the infection, she kept popping more and more of the good white balloons until they were all gone as well. They were keeping the red balloons in balance until they were all gone. Now, all that was left was the resistant red balloons. Now, if those balloons were real bacteria, they could replicate and flourish, causing a worse infection than was present at the beginning!

A scientist, who was present during the Dr. Oz probiotic demo, said that the CDC (Center for Disease Control) researchers have understood for years that it is always best to stop an antibiotic when your symptoms resolve, not necessarily when the antibiotic that was prescribed is all gone! Taking an antibiotic too long contributes to the development of antibiotic resistance.

Using antibacterial hand sanitizers, soaps and household cleaners create resistance as well, and many are made with toxic ingredients.

Finally, in the fall of 2016, the FDA issued a ban on the use of triclosan, triclocarban and 17 other chemicals in hand and body washes. *"Consumers don't need to use antibacterial soaps, and some of them may even be dangerous," the Food and Drug Administration says.* [30]

However, notice this ban says hand and body washes; **triclosan** is still allowed in your toothpaste! The ban also applies only to consumer products, not to antibacterial soaps used in hospitals and food service settings!

The mere thought of **MRSA** (methicillin resistant staph aureus) and "C. diff' (*Clostridium difficile*), strikes fear into the hearts of medical professionals, who understand the deadly health consequences of these resistant bacteria. Nothing can kill these bacteria. Severe, persistent skin disease or unrelenting diarrhea with abdominal pain causes those affected to suffer miserably. Infections with these organisms has become epidemic in our hospitals today. The primary culprit in the development of these infections is the overuse of antibiotics and antibacterials in society with the subsequent proliferation of resistant bacteria, of those red balloons! [31]

So, don't be a germaphobe! Dr. Josh Axe, one of today's popular natural medicine doctors, chiropractor and author wrote in his book, *Eat Dirt*, "Soil based organisms (SBOs) support gut health and immune response….SBOs help plants grow…just as plants grow best in healthy soil teeming with highly active microorganisms, you , too, need these…"

So, do not try to destroy all these natural microbes with harsh, chemical cleaners. A little plain soap and water is fine.

What can you do to promote good bacteria in your environment besides eating dirt? Get a pet!

For those friends and relatives of yours that think your dog is disgusting, or blame cats for harboring disease, Dr. Axe has this to say, "An animal that plays in the dirt brings diverse microbes into the home, some of which the kids may breathe in and others that enter through the skin from touching their furry friends. These microexposures…. add up and help populate the good microbes in your gut…"

Research backs up his assertion that dirty pets are good for us! A study found that children who had cats had a 48 percent decrease in allergies and those with dogs had a 50 percent decrease in allergies. [32]

You can also eat foods which contain bacteria, and other good microbes, such as yeast. **Fermented foods** have been used by societies for hundreds of years as a source of great nutrition and microbes. This practice began when refrigeration was not available. Recently I was reminded in my practice just how effective good quality sauerkraut can be for gut health.[33]

I had watched Dr. Axe's animated video which brilliantly explained leaky gut. He listed several important components to healing the gut and one was sauerkraut. I had worked on one of our resident felines for almost a year with severe blow out diarrhea. We thought we had tried everything, holistic and allopathic. Nothing worked! It was cow plop style and odiferous is putting it mildly. I was so excited to try the sauerkraut on this cat that I grabbed the fresh, organic option which I had in my house, even though it was jalapeno flavor; I was determined to give this a try. Amazingly, Arty loved it! We put a one ml squirt of the kraut juice into his food and in two days, yes, two days this cat passed formed stool. To this day, over six months later, he has formed stool routinely unless we run out of his sauerkraut! I think it is important to say that he had been receiving a variety of other commercial probiotic products with no success. This has become a common recommendation for me when I have a dog or cat patient for whom I suspect leaky gut. I am happy to say I have had amazingly positive feedback on this approach.[34]

Now, I share this advice with the pet parents whom I coach as well. So, you should eat at least a teaspoon of this kraut daily!

Hormones in your food (rBGH/IGF-1)

Most dairy contains bovine growth hormone (rBGH) unless the label says it does not.

Recombinant bovine growth hormone (rBGH) is a synthetic (man-made) hormone that is marketed to dairy farmers to increase milk production in cows. It has been used in the United States since it was approved by the (FDA) in 1993, but its use is not permitted in the European Union, Canada, and some other countries.

BGH is made by the pituitary gland and promotes growth and cell replication. It is the natural form of this hormone in cattle. Recombinant bovine growth hormone (rBGH) is made in a lab using genetic technology. Both the natural and recombinant forms of the hormone stimulate a cow's milk production by increasing levels of another hormone known as insulin-like growth factor (IGF-1). [35]

Studies have found that IGF-1 levels at the high end of the normal range may influence the development of certain tumors. Some early studies found a relationship between blood levels of IGF-1 and the development of prostate, breast, colorectal, and other cancers.

Many people avoid drinking milk or eating yogurt or ice cream as they do not want to ingest this added hormone. What can you choose instead? Drink delicious coconut or almond milk!

Pesticides in your food

Pesticides accumulate in our bodies over time. Organ systems struggle to rid our bodies of pesticides.
Ninety-nine percent of mothers' milk in the United States contains dangerous levels of dichlorodiphenyltrichloroethane (DDT). We all have measurable levels of polychlorinated biphenyls (PCBs), dioxin, heptachlor, chlordane, aldrin, dieldrin, and other pesticides in our bloodstream. These toxins weaken our endocrine, reproductive, circulatory, immune, and central nervous systems. Today's infants have been identified with an average of over 200 toxins in their umbilical cords at birth! Their mothers are so toxic these poisons are being passed through the placentas to the babies even before birth. [36]

Pesticide toxins weaken our organ systems.

Weakened organ systems increase our risk for:
- 🐾 infection
- 🐾 allergy
- 🐾 heart disease
- 🐾 cancer
- 🐾 infertility, miscarriage, and birth defects.

Cancer in Your Pets and You

This pesticide category could not possibly pertain more to you and your pet. I used to see two cases of cancer per year. Now, I see two or more cases per day! Studies have identified more toxins in a pet's blood than in the blood of the human in the same household. Your pet is the canary in the coal mine!
Lawn treatments are NOT gone when it is dry! That belief is plain silly! Do you let your pet or child walk on a treated lawn when the sign is removed? How do you think the chemicals have a residual weed killing effect if they are all gone? Do you think it is okay to smoke or smoke outside?
Pets are susceptible to second and third hand smoke!
Pets have more nasal receptors than we do!
Pets step and roll in things and lick their paws and fur.
This includes our lawns, our clothes and our phones and laptops and our chemical-laden flooring.
Even today's apples are not like yesterday's apples! Do you still think that it is adequate to rinse an apple to remove pesticides? There is big trouble on the inside!

I am continually amazed and saddened by the number of pets who have a family member with a similar cancer. How can this be? Pet and family all share a household with the same energy. Perhaps they all live under the same adverse electromagnetic waves. Maybe they all reside on top of the same toxic landfill. Or sadly, maybe it is a toxic emotional environment that is causing family and pet illness.

Genetically Modified Organisms (GMOs)

So many people just do not understand the significance of this problem. GMOs are plants or animals that have had their DNA modified. In the US, most of the corn, soybean, cotton, and canola crops are now genetically modified. One or more of these can be found in nearly every processed food. [38]

Is this modification a problem? Yes, the reason for the modification and the resulting toxicity is a problem. The modified seed grows a plant that will not die when it is growing in a field next to weeds which are all sprayed with Round-up (glyphosate). The deadly herbicide kills the weeds, but not the modified grain because it is now resistant. This modified plant now contains the herbicide. GMO foods have herbicides and pesticides inside of them! Even the supposedly healthy veggie burger is commonly made with GMO wheat and/or GMO soy.

So, who cares about GMO? Monsanto does! They want you to eat their GMO products!
Monsanto is the agribusiness responsible for the production of these tainted seeds. When you eat a GMO food (corn, potato, canola oil, etc.) the pesticide or herbicide is taken up by your gut flora/good bacteria/microbiome. The pesticide becomes incorporated into your gut wall. (Remember, 80% of your immune system resides in your gut!)

Could this contribute to inflammatory bowel disease? Repetitive inflammation? Gastrointestinal cancer? Hmm, I wonder.

Can GMOs be used in organic products?

The use of genetically modified organisms (GMOs) is prohibited in organic products.

This means an organic farmer cannot plant GMO seeds, an organic cow can't eat GMO alfalfa or corn, and an organic soup producer can't use any GMO ingredients.

Organic farmers and processors must show they are not using GMOs and that they are protecting their products from contact with prohibited substances from farm to table.

Organic Certification Requirements [38]
☐ Land must have had no prohibited substances applied to it for at least 3 years before the harvest of an organic crop.
☐ Soil fertility and crop nutrients will be managed …and allowed synthetic materials.
☐ Crop pests, weeds, and diseases will be controlled primarily through …and biological controls. When these practices are not sufficient, a biological, botanical, or synthetic substance approved for use … may be used.
☐ Operations must use organic seeds and other planting stock when available.
☐ The use of genetic engineering, ionizing radiation and sewage sludge is prohibited.

☐ Animals for slaughter must be raised under organic management from the last third of gestation, or no later than the second day of life for poultry.
☐ Must feed 100 percent organic, …may also provide allowed vitamin and mineral supplements.
☐ Dairy animals must be managed organically for at least 12 months.
☐ All organic livestock are required to have access to the outdoors year-round.
☐ Animals must not be given hormones to promote growth or antibiotics for any reason.
☐ Multi-Ingredient products must have at least 95 percent certified organic content.

☐ "Made with" organic must have at least 70 percent certified organic content. The USDA organic seal may not be used on these products.

So, organic *usually* means antibiotic- free, hormone- free, pesticide- free, non-GMO and pasture time for livestock and poultry! Products which specifically state pasture-raised and organic are best!

✓ Cooked meat, processed meat, charred meat

Step 5: Identify, Avoid, and Replace Processed Meats

> The National Institute of Health (NIH) published a great study that no one (except vegetarians) likes to talk about. In a nutshell it clearly asserts that the more cooked a meat is the more it produces heterocyclic amines. Heterocyclic amines are carcinogenic. Cooked meats cause many types of cancer in humans and animals. Should humans or animals eat *cooked* meat? I think not. But that is up to you. [39]

✓ Coffee

Step 6: Identify, Avoid, and Replace Toxic Coffee and Excessive Caffeine

So, what is so bad about coffee? "Don't take my Starbucks away," you say! Not only is coffee a source of caffeine, but it is a source of chemical residues due to solvent extraction and decaffeination makes this matter worse! However, this is where bioindividuality matters and there are some coffee options that are much better than others, perhaps making coffee even beneficial! Yay!

Caffeine is contained in coffee and in processed tea bags. Caffeine is not present in most organic teas, in particular green tea, which is actually a healthful antioxidant. Natural caffeine from coffee, cocoa, or tea in moderation (1-3 small cups per week) is fine for most people.

Why has caffeine become such a problem? It is found in so many items and has been abused. Caffeine is an additive in soda, gum, diet pills, and pain relievers.
It is an addictive stimulant. It causes calcium to be excreted from the bones, which can lead to osteoporosis. It may decrease fertility. At high doses, caffeine may even cause birth defects, miscarriage, heart disease, depression, behavioral changes, and insomnia. Withdrawal symptoms include headaches, irritability, sleepiness, and lethargy.

There are some great ways for you to avoid or replace caffeine. Substitution always helps with an addiction, but be sure the substitution is a better choice!

Do NOT replace regular coffee with decaf!
The chemical residues left in your coffee
due to the decaffeination process are
worse for you than is the caffeine! Instead,
replace with healthy tea,
mushroom blend drinks, antioxidant, or
B-vitamin drinks!

The best non-coffee substitution that I have found is called
Dandy™ Blend. I drink this almost every day, especially in the
winter. I often combine it with some of David Wolfe's
fabulous, powdered cacao and vanilla stevia or I add his cacao
and mushroom blend to the Dandy Blend. [40, 41]
It tastes remarkably like a real cup of coffee. It dissolves
instantly in hot or cold liquid. I usually add it to hot almond
or coconut milk. Dandy™ Blend is caffeine free with no
acidity or bitterness. It is the only herbal coffee I know of that
includes health benefits of dandelion root and the flavor and
texture of coffee. Personally, I like it better than coffee. In
addition to dandelion, it is made of water-soluble extracts of
roasted roots of chicory and beets, and the grains of barley
and rye. Despite that, it contains no gluten! The company
explains, "*Gluten, which is comprised of proteins that are not
water-soluble, is left behind in the grounds to be composted during
the extracting process, leaving Dandy Blend gluten-free!*"

Fructose, which occurs naturally in the roots of dandelion and
chicory, provides the perception of some sweetness.
According to the manufacturer, there are over 50 trace
minerals in each cup. The company claims there are no
headaches when switching from coffee to Dandy™ Blend.

Is there such a thing as "good for you" real coffee? Dave Asprey invented Bullet Proof Coffee! [42] He lost 100 pounds and increased his energy. He says it is the mold in coffee beans causing the supposed caffeine side effects! Asprey adds coconut oil, or MCT oil (medium chain triglycerides) , to properly prepared ground coffee beans to produce a healthful coffee. This is an addition of a healthy fat. This is consistent with principles of a ketogenic diet. It is all the rave in Hollywood! I learned about this at the David Wolfe Longevity Conference in California. If you can ever make it to one of his events, I highly recommend attending!

✓ Synthetic Vitamins and Minerals

Step 7: Identify, Avoid, and Replace Synthetic Vitamins and Minerals

Just as our pet foods may say natural with added vitamins and minerals, so it is for our foods. In fact, forever we have accepted "fortified" with added vitamins and minerals as a good thing. Not so. Here is why…

Natural vs. Synthetic Vitamins Battling for Cell Receptors
Natural vitamins were discovered. Synthetic vitamins were invented. The vitamin theory began evolving in the early 1900's.
Scientists realized that there were certain deficiency states that could be cured by the addition of particular foods. It did not take long for researchers to try to isolate specific nutrients from the foods which seemed to have the greatest impact on correcting the deficiency state. Synthetics are generally vitamin fractions, not the entire whole food complex intended by nature to be utilized by the body. [43]

Historical Development of Synthetics

In 1906 scientists proposed the existence of thiamin (vitamin B1) and in 1926 it was isolated. In 1932 the structure was determined and in 1933 synthesis was achieved. [44] Why? To sell it of course!

Monetary gain has been a major driving force of the American entrepreneurial spirit and is responsible for many scientific developments. The development of synthetic vitamins and the inclusion of them in processed foods, otherwise devoid of vitamins, has been a life-saving fortification. However, what we now realize is that going back to nature, and consuming real food as a source of our vitamins, is much wiser than reliance on artificial versions of vital nutrients. [45]

Natural are More Effective

We were warned about the use of synthetic vitamins by, ironically of all sources, the authors of an article published in the Journal of the American Medical Association (AMA) as early as 1942! They stated, *"The treatment of scurvy by giving 50 cc. of lemon juice containing 25 mg. of ascorbic acid produces quicker results than 25 mg. of ascorbic acid administered as a medicament. The artificial vitamins, especially vitamin C, are quickly absorbed and also quickly excreted by the kidney. These vitamins have to be administered every day in order to be efficacious. Besides, there exists an antagonism among the different artificial vitamins."* [46]

Obviously, the preceding was written before the corruption of the AMA by Big Pharma.

Natural are Safer

The natural consumption of species-appropriate diets provides checks and balances. This same JAMA source stated that, "*The body eliminates, for instance, vitamin C if vitamin A or D is administered simultaneously.*"[46] *German authors in 1936 explained that "by simultaneous supply of water-soluble (Bs and C) and fat-soluble vitamins (ADEK) together, a hypervitaminosis cannot be produced, though they may be given in very large quantities.*"[47]

Recently a Dogs Naturally facebook discussion enumerated pet guardian concerns regarding various vitamin toxicities, in particular vitamin A. It is clear that toxicities are a concern when utilizing synthetic vitamin sources, but not so when real food is being consumed.

Manufacturers of whole food vitamin supplements commonly explain the synthetic vitamin toxicity phenomenon in this way: Our bodies are made up of millions of cells with receptors on them. The receptors are like a lock and key mechanism. Just the right key will unlock the lock, but the wrong key may go into the lock, but be incomplete in its ability to open the lock and may even get stuck.
Synthetic vitamins may have an initial positive influence on the deficiency state, but repetitive use will result in a negative impact. Synthetic vitamins do not fit properly, and they do not release properly. They gum up the receptors. Then, the for real, complete vitamin complexes cannot act appropriately. It is interesting that a deficiency state of a given vitamin often manifests symptomatically like the toxic state, exhibited by that same vitamin. This is because the repetitive presence or large amount of a vitamin causes the "down regulation" of the vitamin receptors on the cells.
That synthetic vitamin might as well not be there, because it cannot unlock the lock properly, and it does not allow any real vitamin complexes, which may be present, to access the lock or the receptor.

171

Vitamins Need Food to Work

In 1942 a rat experiment proved the previous assertions. Vitamin D deficiency causes rickets, a malformation in bone development. When female rats were fed a vitamin D deficient diet their offspring suffered abnormal bony development. When these rats were fed the diet with added synthetic vitamin D, congenital malformations still occurred in about one third of the offspring. When the same females were fed added liver (as a whole food source of vitamin D) the offspring were normal. [48]

Another poor group of rats were fed fat, intentionally lacking in vitamin A. To this was added pure carotene, extracted from carrots. (Many manufacturers consider carotene equivalent to vitamin A.) These rats developed an eye disease called xerophthalmia. When a similar group of rats were fed the deficient fat with a crude extract of dried carrot, they were protected from the eye disease. Once again, it was demonstrated that a complete food is necessary to provide all constituents of a vitamin complex to prevent or manage disease. [49]

Let's talk B-vitamins. Rabbits lacking B-vitamins developed cirrhosis of the liver. Adding vitamins B1, B2, B3 and B6 did not prevent the disorder. However, when the rabbits were fed yeast, known to be a good source of complete B-vitamin complexes, the condition was prevented. [50]

Many pet guardians believe ascorbic acid is synonymous with vitamin C. It is not. Here is some evidence that it is not. Guinea pigs are highly susceptible to vitamin C deficiency. *"It was demonstrated that guinea pigs, fed vitamin C-free diets, could be more thoroughly protected against infections with pneumococci by lemon juice or orange juice than by pure ascorbic acid."*[47]

Where do synthetic and natural vitamins come from? [51, 52]

Vitamin A

Synthetic vitamin A is called retinyl palmitate or retinyl acetate. It can be made from combining fish or palm oil with beta-ionone. Beta-ionone is manufactured utilizing citrus, acetone, and calcium oxide. Excessive palm oil usage is leading to deforestation of the rainforests and endangerment of orangutans.

Natural vitamin A begins in food as a natural chemical constituent called beta-carotene. The body must convert it into vitamin A to be useful. Vitamin A can be toxic in large doses. Beta-carotene or provitamin A is a precursor which limits the body to convert only what it needs, and to clear what it does not need! This is a natural safeguard against excess and toxic damage. This only works if natural beta-carotene from a whole food source is consumed.

There is an abundance of beta-carotene or provitamin A in yellow and orange fruits and vegetables, dark, leafy greens, and in cod liver oil, liver, egg yolk, butter and cream. I would caution against the use of butter and cream for your dog as a source, due to this species susceptibility to pancreatitis. However, I would highly recommend the provision of the rest of this delicious list of vitamin A sources for your canine carnivore! Remember, mimic the pre-digestion which occurs in the gut of a prey. Steam and blend the dark, leafy greens before feeding. Feed amounts of fruits that would mimic that procured during foraging.

Provide the egg… organic and raw! Be sure the cod liver oil has been distilled in such a way as to have preserved the natural vitamin A, *not* the addition of a synthetic!

Here is an upsetting twist. There is a natural and a synthetic form of beta-carotene! A new study suggests, "*smokers who took beta-carotene supplements in recent experiments may have faced a greater risk of lung cancer because they took the synthetic form of the nutrient. The subtle differences between synthetic and natural beta-carotene do appear to influence how the body uses the nutrient.*

Synthetic beta-carotene consists of just the "all-trans" isomer of the nutrient, whereas natural beta-carotene consists of two different isomers, "9-cis" and "all-trans." Isomers have the same molecular formula, but a different arrangement of atoms. They're a little like anagrams, in which the letters of one word can be rearranged to form another, such as "star" and "rats."
It turns out that the natural 9-cis isomer is a more potent antioxidant than the all-trans. That means the natural form has something the synthetic does not. [53]

What does this mean for your dog? Sadly, dogs do get lung cancer, and commonly and unfairly from third hand smoke! This means from smoke residues on the guardian's clothing. When attempting to choose an antioxidant treatment for your pet, it will be difficult to tell by reading the label if the beta-carotene is natural or synthetic. It is likely always best if all ingredients are derived from real, whole foods.

Vitamin B

Synthetic vitamin B1 is called thiamine monohydrate, thiamine mononitrate, or thiamine hydrochloride.

Industry makes this from coal tar, ammonia, acetone, and hydrochloric acid. Another source utilizes sodium hydroxide and acetone to liberate crystalline thiamine. [54] It is crystalline in structure, unlike plant-based, real vitamins. Many synthetic vitamins are crystalline. Crystals in our blood stream cause damage and mineral accumulation in locations like joints. Thiamine mononitrate and thiamine hydrochloride are regarded as skin and eye irritants. Based on published literature, thiamine should be considered as a sensitizer. [55] Synthetic Vitamin B1 is much less absorbable than natural, because the synthetic is not bound to phosphate. Phosphate binding improves absorption.

Natural vitamin B1 or thiamin is classified as a water-soluble vitamin. It is found in plants and is bound to phosphate. Digestion of the plants releases the thiamin using specialized enzymes that target phosphate. [56]

Synthetic vitamin B2 or riboflavin is made with acetic acid and nitrogen or using genetically modified bacteria and fermentation. It has been shown to be less absorbable and then *quickly removed* from the blood stream and expelled in urine, as if it were a toxin.

Natural vitamin B2 also called riboflavin, is easily absorbed, *stays in the blood stream for long periods* of time, and is readily used by the body as a component of many important enzymes.

Synthetic vitamin B3 or nicotinic acid is manufactured using coal tar, ammonia, acids, 3-cyanopyridine, and formaldehyde. It is less absorbable and has more risks of side effects.

Natural vitamin B3 is called niacinamide or nicotinamide. This is found in food and commonly call niacin. Niacin can have side effects, but these are minimal when coming from plant foods. High dose isolated niacin is no longer recommended for lowering cholesterol as many human patients have suffered serious side effects, such as liver damage, gout, or ulcers.

Synthetic vitamin B5 or pantothenic acid utilizes isobutyraldehyde and formaldehyde to form a calcium (calcium pantothenate) or sodium salt.

Natural vitamin B5 is produced naturally but not stored in the body, so mammals must obtain vitamin B5 from food or supplements each day. Pantothenic acid is easily obtained from many foods but the vitamin is usually **lost in the heating or freezing process**. Vinegar and baking soda can destroy the vitamin. Whole food vitamin B5 is found in most meats, egg yolks, saltwater fish, liver, kidney, vegetables, whole grains, royal jelly, and legumes. Grains are not always a good source, as a large amount of the pantothenic acid is lost during the milling process. Quality yogurt may be a good source of B5.[56] It may be important to supplement fresh food sources of this vitamin for dogs and cats who are consuming frozen raw diets.

Synthetic vitamin B6 or pyridoxine hydrochloride, comes from petroleum ester, hydrochloric acid, and formaldehyde. It isn't readily absorbed or converted and has been shown to actually inhibit the action of natural B6 in the body. It also has side effects not normally found with natural food sources of this vitamin.

Natural vitamin B6 or pyridoxine is bound with phosphate in plants (like bananas) to make pyridoxal-phosphate. Just as we discussed with vitamin B1, this is the biologically active form. Other forms of B6 must be converted into this phosphate form before our body can absorb it.

Synthetic vitamin B7 (biotin) is produced using fumaric acid.[57]

Natural vitamin B7 or biotin is involved in cell growth, fat production, and metabolism. It is also called vitamin H; remember this, as it can improve hair growth. Symptoms of biotin deficiency include thinning hair and brittle nails. Raw egg white contains a substance that binds biotin in the intestine and keeps it from being absorbed. Eating two or more uncooked egg whites daily for several months has caused biotin deficiency that is serious enough to produce symptoms. So feed the whole egg! Egg yolk is a great source of biotin! Isn't that interesting? Other sources include liver and Swiss chard. [57]

Synthetic vitamin B9 or folic acid comes from petroleum derivatives, acids, and acetylene. It does not exist at all in natural foods. It is crystalline and is not easily absorbed. Large amounts are put into supplements.

Natural vitamin B9 is called folate. It is important to the development and repair of DNA. Many women recognize the importance of consuming this during pregnancy for the development of a healthy baby.

Synthetic vitamin B12 is derived by fermenting cobalt and cyanide to make cyanocobalamin.

Natural vitamin B12, or cobalamin, is only created by micro-organisms. Good bacteria (probiotics) that flourish in our intestines or grow in soil can produce cobalamin. Some micro-algae and some seaweed species can produce cobalamin as well. This is especially important for vegetarians, in particular vegans to be aware as to the limited resources available for procurement of this important vitamin.

Synthetic choline as choline chloride or choline bitartrate is made using ethylene, ammonia, and hydrochloric acid or tartaric acid. It is not bound to phosphate. It is usually included in the B vitamin category.

Natural choline is combined with phosphate in nature and is important to cell membrane structure and fat metabolism.

Vitamin C

Synthetic vitamin C or ascorbic acid is isolated from genetically modified corn sugar that is hydrogenated and processed with acetone. Ascorbic acid is crystalline. It does not include the flavonoids and phytonutrients that make it work. Beware of products called *rose hips vitamin C* as they can legally mix pure crystalline ascorbic acid with a pinch of rose hips and say "all-natural" since there is no legal definition of this. [45]

Natural vitamin C as a whole food complex is found in citrus, red bell peppers, berries, and of course, many more fruits and vegetables. In nature it is combined with flavonoids and phytonutrients that help in its absorption and use.

Synthetic vitamin D is produced from the irradiation of animal fat. This stimulates vitamin D3 synthesis. Lanolin is the waxy secretion from sheep skin which is commonly used as the fat source.

Natural vitamin D3 can be made by our own body fat when we expose our skin to sunlight. Many mushrooms and yeast produce vitamin D2 when exposed to sunlight. Lichens also produce vitamin D3, which is the most effective kind. Beware of any vitamin D2 supplements as these are ineffective. Vitamin D3 is actually a downstream metabolite of cholesterol. It is more of a hormone, than it is strictly a vitamin. Vitamin D deficiency is epidemic and correlates with depressed mood and the presence of many cancers.

Synthetic vitamin E termed dl-alpha tocopherol is created using refined oils, trimethylhydroquinone, and isophytol. It is not as easily absorbed, does not stay as long in tissues, and is quickly dispelled like a toxin or unknown chemical.

Natural vitamin E refers to 8 different fat-soluble compounds and it acts as an antioxidant that protects fats from oxidation. The most biologically active form is found in grains, seeds, and the oils derived from grains and seeds.
I commonly recommend Standard Process Wheat Germ Oil as a whole food source of Vitamin E. In this form it is complexed with selenium and other important components which make it utilizable by the body. The d-alpha tocopherol commonly touted as natural vitamin E is not a whole food complex either. I recommend this product only be used topically, on incisions for example. It is not my go-to oral product. If a vitamin is whole food, a lesser amount of IU's or milligrams will get the job done better than a greater concentration of a synthetic version. Therefore dosing recommendations of vitamins can be very misleading.

Synthetic vitamin K is also called menadione sodium bisulfate, sodium bisulfate, or vitamin K3. It is inexpensive and can be dangerous. It may have carcinogenic effects and can be toxic to kidneys, lungs, liver and mucous membranes.

Repeated use can cause organ damage. [45]

Veterinarians administer an injection or capsules of K1 (not the synthetic K3) to a pet who has consumed rat poison. The poison causes internal bleeding, prevention of clotting. Vitamin K is the antidote.

Natural vitamin K is found in dark leafy greens. Alfalfa and kelp are commonly provided as supplements and are great natural sources of whole food vitamin K. This vitamin is important to proper blood clotting and some other metabolic pathways.

✓ Toxic Packaging

Step 8: Identify, Avoid, and Replace Plastics and Aluminum bisphenol-A (BPA)

Resin linings of most tin cans contain BPA, a synthetic estrogen. It has been linked to reproductive problems, heart disease, diabetes, and obesity. Acidity, from tomatoes for example, causes BPA to leach into the canned product. BPA in most individuals exceeds the amount that suppresses sperm production or causes chromosomal damage to the eggs of animals. So, toxic packaging and processing is another reason you should avoid processed foods. [59]

HPP (high pressure pasteurization)
Some foods are pressurized inside a plastic bag to kill bacteria. It is now by-law, BPA free, however I would ask, what other yet unidentified plastic toxins should we be concerned about? Are we trading our concerns regarding bacteria for the ingestion of plastic toxins?

What is my solution? Again, identify, avoid, and replace the best you can! **Purchase or store your items in glass or stainless steel whenever possible.** Especially use glass or stainless steel if you are adding essential oils to water or other liquids held in these containers. Please avoid aluminum and any plastic. Essential oils will literally pull these toxins from the bottle into the liquid. If you need to use plastic, always choose BPA free. Purchase all tomato products in glass!

How Many Toxins Can You Count?

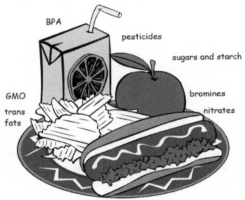

Photo pixabay.com

Do not let your pet see you eating the SAD diet! Live with your pet in mind. If you have no one else to hold you accountable, let it be your pet! Take charge of your life because you care about yourself and your pet. Love yourself as much as you love your pet! Start today!

Action Plan

- 🖐 Drink lots of purified water or spring water to flush toxins from your body. Add Celtic sea salt?
- 🖐 Use fresh raw vegetable juices to detox and provide whole food source vitamins, minerals, antioxidants!
- 🖐 Sleep at least 8-9 hours per day to strengthen your body's immune system.

- Exercise to relax your body and mind and to build muscle for strength and detoxification.
- Watch less television to decrease your exposure to processed food advertising and negative thinking.
- Shop the grocery store perimeter! Eat a variety of fresh, healthy foods in order to stay out of the hospital!
- Choose organic! (milk, orange juice, strawberries, potatoes, tomatoes, especially!)
- Read ingredient labels and look for the easy to recognize seals for organic, non-GMO, GF (gluten free) no BGH, and even the bunny for cruelty-free!
- Replace poor eating habits!
- Learn to cook at home!
- Make the time!

Make the Time, Shop Fresh, Cook at Home

Start by adding one simple new recipe to your routine menu every week. Here is one of my favorites! You can purchase these items at most common grocery stores. If you cannot find them, ask! This is remarkably quick to put together and you can prepare it in advance and refrigerate it.

Winter Holiday Salad Recipe
(This is very pretty!)
Quinoa, kale, goji berry

Ingredients:
1 cup cooked, cooled quinoa
1 large bunch curly leaf kale, trimmed into strips and sautéed in raw butter

¾ cup of re-hydrated Young Living®(YL) goji berries
1 cup (Go Raw™) sprouted pumpkin/sunflower seeds or
another crunch that you prefer, lightly toasted in butter
6 tablespoons extra-virgin olive oil
2 tablespoons apple cider vinegar
2 teaspoons Brennan's Dusseldorf mustard or your favorite
Add to taste Power Blend™ Garlic Sea Salt or your seasoning
idea
2 drops YL lime oil or tablespoon lemon juice

Directions:
Whisk together the oil, vinegar, mustard and seasonings in a
small bowl.
Mix the quinoa, kale and most of the goji berries in a large
bowl.
Blend the dressing from the small bowl into the salad in the
large bowl and garnish with the rest of the goji berries.
Serves 5 to 8 people. Store covered in frig for a couple days.

Add Healthy Supplements and Essential Oils

Major components missing from a processed diet:
☐ Probiotics, consider Young Living (YL) Life 9
   (sauer kraut, kefir, kimchi, kombucha)
☐ Enzymes, consider YL Detoxyme (separate from meals) or
Essentialzymes-4 (with meal)
☐ Whole Food vitamins, consider YL Multigreens or Standard
Process (SP) Cruciferous Complete or SP Green Food
☐ Omega 3 Fatty Acids, consider OmegaGize or Nordic
Naturals or Standard Process fish oils (Quality is important!)

Does this look familiar? This was the same list of missing
nutrient categories in processed foods fed to your pet. This is a
simple check off list of a place to start for you! Don't be
overwhelmed. Small changes can make a big difference!

Primary vs. Secondary Foods

**© 2005 Integrative Nutrition Inc. © 2013 Integrative Nutrition Inc.
(used with permission)**

There is way more to self-care than the food that you put on
your plate and the supplements that you put into your mouth.
During my one year of study to receive a certificate as an
Integrative Nutrition® Health Coach, I learned that these
foods are only Secondary Foods. According to my instructor,
Joshua Rosenthal, "the Primary Foods are lifestyle factors that
create optimal health. Four types are: relationships, physical
activity, career and spirituality."

Recognize that your Primary Foods are just as, maybe even
more important than your Secondary Foods. This recognition
will greatly impact your emotional and physical health.

Remember, Secondary Foods are what you put on your plate
and into your mouth. Primary Foods encompass some things
that come out of your mouth!

These facets of your life may be healthy or toxic, just like
Secondary Foods. The Circle of Life is a great IIN® (Institute
for Integrative Nutrition®) tool that is used by health coaches
to explain the Primary Foods. You can use it to check in on
yourself. Use the following exercise to recognize how
balanced your life is in regard to these Primary Food
categories.

The Circle of Life

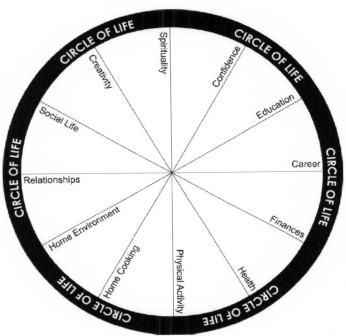

©   **2005**

Integrative Nutrition Inc. (used with permission)

The Circle of Life exercise will help you to discover which primary foods you are missing the most. The Circle of Life has 12 sections. Look at each section and place a dot on the line marking how satisfied you are with each area of your life. A dot placed at the center of the circle or close to the middle indicates dissatisfaction, while a dot placed on the periphery indicates ultimate happiness. When you have placed a dot on each of the lines, connect the dots to see your circle of life. You will have a clear visual of any imbalances in primary food and a starting point for determining where you may wish to spend more time and energy to create balance and joy in your life.

You can control your management and perception of these life components. Perception is reality. You can choose to care for your mind, body, and spirit in a positive way, regardless of your surroundings.

Being mindful of your Primary and Secondary Foods is important to proper self-care. Successful self-care, making good, positive choices, will impact your mood. Your mood affects everyone around you including your pet. What you believe, will transpire. "Fake it til you make it" might sound cliché, but as simplistic as it sounds, it is often the most profoundly important thing each of us can do daily to survive and thrive in this difficult world!

Energy Healing Modalities

A great way to elevate your mood is with any of the many energy healing modalities. Breath work, yoga, massage, acupuncture and essential oils all take into consideration the healing power of oxygen and balancing frequencies.

We are all composed of energy. Surrounding yourself with positive energy can uplift you. In the same way, negative energy can bring you down. We have all experienced that who we hang with can bring us up or down. How can you use a natural modality to do the same?

Essential Oils for You

Essential oils possess energy frequencies which can elevate or calm. There is a single oil or an oil blend to support almost any situation. Oils can be diffused for aromatherapy, applied topically, and in many cases used internally.

Lavender

What if you are all keyed up at bedtime and you just can't relax to sleep? I am sure you have heard that **lavender** oil can calm you so that you can rest. You can put five drops in a warm bath with a healthy soap and some Epsom or Himalayan salts. Maybe you're like me and you just don't love the smell of lavender. There are other options.

Stress Away™

I have a relaxing blend of oils in a roll-on. I apply this blend to my neck every morning to take away my stressful thoughts. This blend contains: vanilla, lime, copaiba, cedarwood, ocotea and lavender. Powerful constituents in this blend include cedrol and eugenol. Google plant constituents to learn more.

Joy™ and Rose

If I am a little sad or I just want to be sure to have a delightful day, the healthy "perfume" that I apply to my wrists contains my favorite oil, **jasmine, blended with bergamot, ylang ylang, geranium, lemon, coriander, tangerine, Roman chamomile, palmarosa and rose.** Rose has an extremely high frequency and I love putting this on "neat", just where my neck meets the back of my head, to raise me to my highest potential!

I truly believe that what my conscious mind says, my unconscious mind believes. This belief manifests as my reality.

So, let's stop sabotaging ourselves with self-deprecating thoughts and talk. Let's strive for our highest potential!

Frankincense and Myrrh

I am sure that it was no accident that the three wisemen brought **frankincense and myrrh** to the baby Jesus king! Many believe the third gift of gold was actually a golden oil, perhaps balsam fir. You can't have a discussion about natural health self-care without a focus on essential oils. These are God-given because they can impact every facet of our being. Oils can bring balance to us emotionally and physically. These oils can enhance beautiful skin and the immune system.

Aromatherapy

Use aromatherapy every day. Diffuse oils which can oxygenate your blood and brain. Increase your focus and clarity. Improve cognition and motivation to achieve your goals. Think about the trees and leaves in our environment and how wonderful a walk in the woods can feel. Inhaling the tree oils can have a similar impact. You will feel strong and uplifted like a tree! Choose cedar wood, black spruce, cypress, or balsam fir.

Internal Oils

Prepare recipes which contain essential oils. Traditional cultures have developed dishes which were delicious and medicinal. Today's society has lost the art of healthy food seasoning. When Hippocrates said, "Let food be thy medicine and medicine be thy food," he was not kidding. As the health coaching movement thrives, so grows the usage of herbs, spices, and essential oils in the American diet. It is once again becoming fun to cook!

Citrus Oils

You can begin simply by putting a couple drops of **lemon** oil into your water each day. Many of the citrus oils can impart a freshness to your day. Place a couple drops of **tangerine**, orange or lime in your water or fruit drink. (Use only glass bottles.) Diffuse a blend of these to make your mind believe your house is clean! When your environment is clean, your mind helps you be more organized in your thinking as well.

Peppermint

Many oils veterans use peppermint topically as a driver layered on top of other oils and apply to the temples. However, do not forget that this oil can be delicious! Treat yourself to some gluten-free brownies with essential oil of **peppermint** added.

Basil

No fresh basil on hand? You can put one toothpick tip of **basil** oil into a tablespoon of olive oil. Use this as dressing with Balsamic vinegar drizzled over tomato and mozzarella slices.

Slique™

Another refreshing blend to mix into your water contains delicious spearmint oil and ocotea, which can help support healthy weight.

There are hundreds of oils from which to choose. Just the thought of selecting a personal oil and experiencing the fragrance can be uplifting! Combine essential oils with other energy modalities such as breath work, yoga, massage, Reiki, or acupuncture and you will catapult your mind-body experience to a whole new level!

LET'S WRAP IT UP

There is more to having a pet companion than just surviving in the same space!

What are the five most powerful influences on your pet's well-being?
1) Your Conscious Language™ and thoughts
2) The food you provide
3) The health care you choose
4) The living environment that you share
5) Your self-care

If you knew what your pet were thinking, would you speak more eloquently and more positively? Would you think differently if you knew your cat had an opinion? If you knew your cat cared, would you feed this best friend processed food or real nourishment? Would you research alternative care options to be sure you are providing the best, up-to-date health care for your precious canine, if you thought he could live better and live longer? If you thought the space that you each share was toxic realistically and figuratively, would you clean it up for your pet's sake and yours? If you knew, really knew, how much your pet loves you, would you take better care of yourself?

If you answered a resounding yes to all these questions, but feel you need help in some of these areas to move forward, there are many excellent resources to guide you in your journey!

Beyond the Book

There are holistic veterinarians and Integrative Nutrition® Health Coaches who are perfectly qualified to help in many of these areas. Reach out to me for a phone consult or search the **www.AHVMA.org** website.

Our current health care system is woefully inadequate. The Institute for Integrative Nutrition® reports:

"Nearly 30% of the world's population is obese or overweight. Less than 1/8 of physical visits include any nutrition counseling. Seventy percent of deaths each year are caused by chronic illness. One in three American adults have high blood pressure and only 3% of our healthcare dollars are spent on preventing diseases."

Please find practitioners, for yourself and your pet, who are trained in the areas which I have discussed in this book.

Please support initiatives which help develop healthier minds and bodies.

My experience at the Institute for Integrative Nutrition® (IIN), where I received my training in holistic wellness and health coaching and my participation in their Launch Your Dream Book course, provided me with the resources and motivation to complete this book, which has been a life time goal.

IIN® provided me with a truly comprehensive Health Coach Training Program which I did not expect, but was pleasantly surprised to receive! I was surprised to learn about much more than physical nourishment!

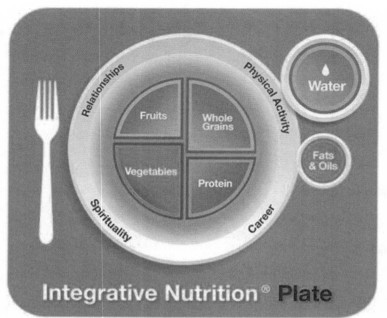

Integrative Nutrition® Plate
© **2012 Integrative Nutrition Inc. (used with permission)**

From the physical aspects of nutrition and eating wholesome foods that work best for each individual person, to the concept of Primary Food – the idea that everything in life including our spirituality, career, relationships, and fitness contribute to our inner and outer health - IIN® has helped me strive for optimal health and balance. **I began the IIN® journey with the passion to learn and share human nutrition with pet parents, but I was further inspired to learn about the Primary Foods and "bioindividuality" in order to have a positive impact on the pet guardians entire holistic experience.**

Beyond personal health, IIN® offers training in health coaching, as well as business and marketing training. Although I came into the course having owned my own business for 25 years, I came away with a multitude of new ideas and techniques for enhancing my current business and relationships. I was excited to take this course and learn from renowned wellness experts with whom I was familiar, such as David Wolfe and Andrew Weil, but I was amazed at the number and caliber of diverse experts and motivational presenters with whom I was totally unfamiliar. I had never heard Deepak Chopra. And Dr. Oz presented a very different outside of his show format. I could listen to Joshua Rosenthal's voice of wisdom every day. During the course, I did! I will miss that!

The convenience of this online learning platform has allowed me to participate in a school program which has changed my life, and I believe it could do the same for you.

Regardless of your specific professional ambition, I invite you to learn more about the Institute for Integrative Nutrition® and even explore the idea of a Health Coach Training Program. It just might transform your life, your relationships and even your pets!

Feel free to contact me to talk more about IIN® at **docjodie@drjodiesnaturalpets.com**, visit www.DrJodiesNaturalPets.com or call (844) 315-8546 to enroll. Tell them Dr. Jodie sent you!

If you would like to continue our conversation beyond the book, follow 'Jodie Gruenstern' on Facebook! Members of my Facebook group, "Pets Have Feelings Too!" have had a lot to post and say in comments regarding this topic as well!

One member posted a CNN story about how pets can comprehend our words and respond to them in an emotional way. A passionate commenter said apparently this is news to CNN, but certainly not to pet lovers!

I would love to meet you personally at a book signing, a class, or one-on-one for a visit with you and your pet! Please contact me by visiting any of my websites to learn more or to schedule an appointment!

As David Wolfe says, *"Have the best day ever!"*

Postscript

If you have read this whole book and say to yourself, "I know all this; I strive to incorporate all these topics into my daily life, but despite that, there is still something missing. My food, family, finances and my pets help me survive, but I am not feelin' the joy!" Then consider these thoughts from a sermon by Pastor Kevin at the Scottsdale Bible Church:

Symptoms of Not Feeling Christ's Love
Emptiness that can only be filled by God
Very unsure, maybe even hate yourself
Constantly looking for approval
Critical of others
Difficulty in relationships
Defined by things outside of us
Never at peace
Addiction, trying to fill an emptiness

We carry the wounds of being unloved in our right brain. **The way we cure this is by being loved.** *Scientists say this above all things, have fervent love for one another. The Bible says when two or three come together healing can occur. At some point on our journey, we must begin to heal and experience the Father's love. It is not the will of God that you should feel empty. He is always there.*

Our pets are so giving. Be careful to not fill your void with only them, Live with Your Pet in Mind. Protect them from your anger, grief, and fears. Find joy. Share the joy with your pets!

NOTES

Introduction

(1) https://www.ncbi.nlm.nih.gov/pubmed/20573797

Chapter 1

(1) Gregg Braden, New York Times best-selling author of: The Divine Matrix, The God Code, Secrets of the Lost Mode of Prayer, and The Isaiah Effect
(2) Life Application Study Bible Tyndale House Publishers 2004
(3) Robert Tennyson Stevens, author of Conscious Language™, The Logos of Now
(4) Robert Tennyson Stevens lecture, Highest Potential Academy 2015

Chapter 2

(1) https://www.youtube.com/watch?v=aA5wAm2c0
   1w
(2) https://en.wikipedia.org/wiki/Telepathy
(3) http://www.smithsonianmag.com/innovation/scie
   ntists-prove-that-telepathic-communication-is-
   within-reach-180952868/?no-ist

Chapter 3

(1) http://www.kindredspiritsanimalcommunication.c
   om/

Chapter 4

(1) http://www.aspca.org/animal-homelessness/shelter-intake-and-surrender/pet-statistics
(2) http://www.humanesociety.org/issues/abuse_neglect/facts/animal_cruelty_facts_statistics.html
(3) http://www.americanhumane.org/position-statement/animal-population-control/

Chapter 5

(1) http://agr.wa.gov/FP/Pubs/docs/092-ProhibitedAnimalProteins.pdf
(2) http://c.ymcdn.com/sites/www.petfoodinstitute.org/resource/collection/3257670C-41DB-4680-81FD-2F1FC78AB5A4/Proposed_Revisions_to_AAFCO_Nutrient_Profiles_051513_Final.pdf
(3) http://www.traciehotchner.com/files/AAFCO-Definitions-of-Dog-Food_Ingredients.pdf
(4) http://www.integrativesystems.org/systems-biology-of-gmos/
(5) http://naturalsociety.com/study-gmo-soy-accumulates-cancer-causing-formaldehyde/
(6) http://www.glutenfreedietitian.com/gluten-free-diet-arsenic-and-rice/
(7) http://www.thekitchn.com/good-grains-what-is-millet-67713
(8) http://www.todaysdietitian.com/newarchives/110211p36.shtml
(9) http://www.livescience.com/36424-food-additive-bha-butylated-hydroxyanisole.html
(10) https://noshly.com/additive/324/antioxidant/324/#approvals

(11) http://natureslogic.blogspot.com/2013/04/what-about-gmos-and-protein.html

(12) http://www.academia.edu/7443850/Glyphosates_Suppression_of_Cytochrome_P450_Enzymes_and_Amino_Acid_Biosynthesis_by_the_Gut_Microbiome_Pathways_to_Modern_Diseases

(13) http://www.prebiotic.ca/chicory_root.html

(14) https://experiencelife.com/article/probiotics-at-work/

(15) http://www.healthline.com/health/food-nutrition/is-red-dye-40-toxic#2

(16) http://www.aafco.org/Consumers/What-is-in-Pet-Food

(17) http://www.rabbit.org/journal/3-3/digestibility.html

(18) www.aafco.org

(19) https://www.ncbi.nlm.nih.gov/pubmed/1500323

(20) http://www.ketopetsanctuary.com/

(21) www.westonaprice.org

(22) http://www.vin.com/apputil/content/defaultadv1.aspx?meta=&pId=11147&id=3846250

(23) https://authoritynutrition.com/resistant-starch-101/

(24) Ferretti and Levandar, 1976

(25) Arciszewskaet al, 1982; Shamberger, 1985; Kramer and Ames, 1988

(26) Merck Index 1983

(27) http://www.cdc.gov/niosh/ipcsneng/neng0698.html

(28) http://ivcjournal.com/whole-food-vitamins/

(29) Fermentation of Fructooligosaccharides and Inulin by Bifidobacteria: a Comparative Study of Pure and Fecal Cultures
http://aem.asm.org/content/71/10/6150.short

(30) Convention Notes Ohio 2016, www.ahvma.org

Chapter 6

(1) http://news.wisc.edu/schultz-dog-vaccines-may-not-be-necessary/
(2) https://vetlabel.com/
(3) https://www.amazon.com/Canine-Thyroid-Epidemic-Answers-Need/dp/1617810169
(4) http://www.ifautoimmunearthritis.org/
(5) http://www.vcahospitals.com/main/pet-health-information/article/animal-health/cushings-disease-in-dogs/545
(6) http://woundeducators.com/systemic-factors-affecting-wound-healing/
(7) In a 2012 interview posted to the DVM 360 website, kidney specialist, Gregory F. Grauer, DVM, MS, DACVIM
(8) Clinical Medicine of the Dog and Cat Iowa State Press Schaer 2003
(9) Journal of Prolotherapy Volume 2 Issue 1 February 2010
(10) Small Animal Surgery Mosby Fossum 1997 p.945
(11) Reference Guide for Essential Oils by Higley
(12) Essential Oils Desk Reference
(13) http://healthypets.mercola.com/sites/healthypets/archive/2011/02/17/dangers-of-early-pet-spaying-or-neutering.aspx

Chapter 7

(1) http://personalmoneystore.com/moneyblog/fda-investigate-triclosan-triclosan-banned-eu/
(2) http://slsfree.net/
(3) http://npic.orst.edu/factsheets/PermGen.html
(4) Reference Guide for Essential Oils by Higley
(5) Essential Oils Desk Reference
(6) Am J Epidemiol 1998; 147:488–92.

(7) Am J Epidemiol 2002; 156:268–73.

Chapter 8

(1) http://www.seattleorganicrestaurants.com/vegan
     -whole-foods/top-10-toxic-foods-preservatives-
     additives/#sthash.PCsZptWX.dpuf
(2) http://articles.mercola.com/sites/articles/archive
     /2009/10/13/artificial-sweeteners-more-
     dangerous-than-you-ever-imagined.aspx
(3) http://www.health.harvard.edu/healthy-
     eating/glycemic_index_and_glycemic_load_for_100_fo
     ods
(4) http://www.livescience.com/36257-aspartame-
     health-effects-artificial-sweetener.html
(5) http://naturalsociety.com/toxin-name-still-
     deadly-fda-changes-aspartames-name-amino-
     sweet/
(6) http://www.medicalnewstoday.com/articles/24460
     3.php
(7) http://ajcn.nutrition.org/content/79/4/537.full
(8) http://circ.ahajournals.org/content/114/6/597
(9) http://www.medicinenet.com/insulin_resistance/art
     icle.htm

(10) http://www.webmd.com/diet/features/the-truth-
     about-agave#1
(11) http://www.steviaparaguaya.com.py/english/hi
     story6.html
(12) http://www.foodrenegade.com/is-truvia-
     healthy/
(13) http://www.fda.gov/downloads/Food/IngredientsP
     ackagingLabeling/GRAS/NoticeInventory/UCM2641
     11
(14) http://www.mayoclinic.org/healthy-
     lifestyle/nutrition-and-healthy-eating/expert-
     answers/bvo/faq-20058236

(15) http://www.iodine-resource.com/halogens.html

(16) http://www.foodnavigator-usa.com/Regulation/FDA-Brominated-vegetable-oil-BVO-is-safe-so-removing-its-interim-status-is-not-a-priority

(17) http://health.usnews.com/health-news/health-wellness/articles/2015/01/16/are-energy-drinks-really-that-bad

(18) https://www.ewg.org/foodnews/dirty_dozen_list.php

(19) https://www.youngliving.com/en_US/products/ningxia-zyng

(20) https://www.youngliving.com/en_US/products/ningxia-nitro

(21) http://www.ncbi.nlm.nih.gov/pubmed/17109576

(22) https://en.wikipedia.org/wiki/Xylitol

(23) http://www.globalhealingcenter.com/natural-health/health-concerns-of-refined-sugar/

(24) http://www.mayoclinic.org/diseases-conditions/high-blood-cholesterol/in-depth/trans-fat/ART-20046114?pg=2

(25) http://www.wheatbellyblog.com/

(26) http://www.westonaprice.org/health-topics/dirty-secrets-of-the-food-processing-industry/

(27) https://en.wikipedia.org/wiki/Butylated_hydroxyanisole

(28) http://www.sciencedirect.com/science/article/pii/S000527289900033X

(29) http://www.dogsnaturallymagazine.com/why-are-pet-foods-making-people-sick/

(30) http://www.beyondpesticides.org/programs/antibacterials/triclosan

(31) http://www.clevelandclinicmeded.com/medical
pubs/diseasemanagement/gastroenterology/anti
biotic-associated-diarrhea/

(32) http://www.webmd.com/hypertension-high-
blood-pressure/features/health-benefits-of-
pets#1

(33) http://wellnessmama.com/2245/health-benefits-
fermented-foods/

(34) https://draxe.com/4-steps-to-heal-leaky-gut-and-
autoimmune-disease/

(35) http://www.cancer.org/cancer/cancercauses/ot
hercarcinogens/athome/recombinant-bovine-
growth-hormone

(36) https://www.niehs.nih.gov/health/topics/agent
s/pesticides/

(37) http://www.nongmoproject.org/learn-
more/what-is-gmo/

(38) https://www.ams.usda.gov/grades-
standards/organic-standards

(39) https://www.cancer.gov/about-cancer/causes-
prevention/risk/diet/cooked-meats-fact-sheet

(40) www.dandyblend.com

(41) www.longevitywarehouse.com

(42) www.bulletproof.com

(43) http://www.sunwarrior.com/news/natural-vs-
synthetic-vitamins/

(44) The Vitamins Third Edition Coombs Jr. Elsevier,
Inc. 2008

(45) http://www.doctorsresearch.com/articles4.html

(46) JAMA, 118, 6:475, February 1942

(47) The Vitamins and their Clinical Applications,
Kuhnau and Schroeder, 1936

(48) JAMA, 118, 12:1002, March 1942

(49) The Vitamins, Sherman and Smith, Monograph
Series, Chemical Catalog Company, 1931

(50) Annual Review of Physiology, Rawkins, 3:259-282, 1941

(51) Eating Well for Optimal Health, Weil, Harper Collins 2001

(52) The Crystal and Molecular Structure of Thiamine Chloride Monohydrate, Acia Cryst. 1972

(53) The Real Truth about Vitamins and Antioxidants, DeCava, Selene River Press 2006

(54) http://www.wisegeekhealth.com/what-is-calcium-pantothenate.htm

(55) American Journal of Clinical Nutrition (May 1996; 63:729-34), Ami Ben-Amotz, Ph.D., and Yishai Levy, Ph.D.

(56) Opinion on the safety and efficacy of vitamin B1 (thiamine mononitrate and thiamine hydrochloride) as a feed additive for all animal species based on a dossier submitted by DSM Nutritional Products. EFSA Journal 2011;9 (11):2413. www.efsa.europa.eu/efsajournal

(57) http://www.nlm.nih.gov/medlineplus/druginfo/natural/313.html

(58) http://en.wikipedia.org/wiki/Biotin

(59) http://www.alternet.org/personal-health/toxic-traps-when-these-7-types-plastic-are-dangerous

INDEX

About the Author

Dr. Jodie and Jetson

Jodie Gruenstern, DVM, CVA is a UW-Madison graduate and began practicing veterinary medicine in Muskego, Wisconsin in 1987. She is a certified veterinary acupuncturist and food therapist by the Chi Institute. She has been a member of the AVMA, AHVMA, WVMA, MVMA, AzVMA, and VP of the VMAA (Veterinary Medical Aromatherapy® Association). Dr. Jodie is former owner of the Animal Doctor Holistic Veterinary Complex. Her facility was awarded Muskego Business of the year in 2013. She is a nationally renowned speaker. She has been an advocate for natural pet care through presenting, radio, and television. She has written for Dogs Naturally Magazine, Innovative Veterinary Care, Animal Wellness, Nature's Pathways and Natural Awakenings. She has appeared on PetMD. Dr. Jodie is an avid supporter of raw diets for dogs and cats. She uses multiple modalities in her integrative practice including no anesthesia teeth cleaning, acupuncture, laser therapy, whole food supplements, essential oils, and western and Chinese herbals.

Dr. Jodie is founder of the non-profit iPAW: Integrating People for Animal Wellness, which supports the needs of pets who might have otherwise been euthanized. Learn more or donate at **www.iPAWaid.com**!

Dr. Jodie is the owner of Dr. Jodie's Natural Pets which manufactures unique natural dog and cat treats and products. Learn more or order retail or wholesale by visiting **www.DrJodiesNaturalPets.com**! Available on Amazon!

Dr. Jodie is former owner of the Animal Doctor Holistic Veterinary Complex in Wisconsin. You can now reach her in Arizona via email. ***docjodie@drjodiesnaturalpets.com***

Dr. Jodie is former Vice President of the Veterinary Medical Aromatherapy Association. You can count on her to educate and promote the safe and efficacious use of high-quality essential oils in animals.

Dr. Jodie is available for email consultations and in Arizona at select locations for holistic pet examinations, veterinary referrals, second opinions, nutritional consultations, and integrative coaching for pet parents.
Email her at **docjodie@drjodiesnaturalpets.com** or visit **https://drjodiesintegrativeconsulting.standardprocess.com/ to set up your own personal account for access to whole food supplements!**

Socialize together on Facebook!
"Friend" or "Follow" Jodie Gruenstern
Dr. Jodie is the administrator for:

* Dr. Jodie's Natural Pets
* Integrating People for Animal Wellness
* Dr. Jodie's Pet SpOilers
* Anesthesia Free Teeth Cleaning Arizona
* Pets Have Feelings Too

Young Living® Essential Oils

Has Dr. Jodie inspired you to live young with oils? Visit
www.docjodie.com for more information or to join her team!
Your fragrant starter kit will arrive with a
FREE diffuser!
Act Today!

"Live with Your Pet in Mind" Philanthropy

One dollar from every book sale is donated to iPAW.
Integrating People for Animal Wellness is a 501c3 dedicated to
the prevention of unwarranted euthanasia by intervening
with housing, funding, and alternative care education. Please
"like" Integrating People for Animal Wellness on Facebook
and visit the website and logo clothing shop at
www.iPAWaid.com!